Also by Benjamin Kaufman:

Pressing On! Why Leaders Derail and What to Do About It

Flourishing In The Ministry

Confronting The Challenges
Facing Young Ministers

By
Benjamin M. Kaufman

With
Drew Smithson & Mike DeVito

WESTBOW
P R E S S
A DIVISION OF THOMAS NELSON

WestBow Press books may be ordered through booksellers or by contacting:

WestBow Press
A Division of Thomas Nelson
1663 Liberty Drive
Bloomington, IN 47403
www.westbowpress.com
1-(866) 928-1240

ISBN: 978-1-4497-3418-3 (sc)
ISBN: 978-1-4497-3419-0 (hc)
ISBN: 978-1-4497-3417-6 (e)

Library of Congress Control Number: 2012900818

Printed in the United States of America

WestBow Press rev. date: 02/10/2012

To Sherie,
my lovely wife
and ministry partner
for twenty-eight years

Table of Contents

Introduction

As a twenty-six-year-old youth pastor on a staff with four other pastors at a San Diego church, I had to climb some ladders to reach the top—literally.

Every Tuesday morning I had to climb a ladder to manually spell out the new announcements on our old-fashioned church marquee (sign). We had a full-time church custodian, Mr. G., but he was in his sixties, and I agreed with others who said that it might have been dangerous for him to climb an eight-foot ladder, so the job fell to the youth pastor—in this case, me. Normally I was quite satisfied to do this job. But a few times my pride cropped up and I found myself thinking that I was really above such a job. And then, a few times I thought, why don't the other guys on staff do this job some time? Once, my inner conversation even turned to sarcasm: *Jesus said that if you want to be great in the kingdom, be the servant of all. So, why can't we pass around this "privilege" of being a servant to others? Why do I always have to be the great one?* Our inner conversations can be amusing, can't they? But, seriously, as I look back, I realize that I learned a lot of lessons about servanthood by climbing that ladder.

The second ladder I climbed was at the same church, in our A-frame sanctuary. Some of the light bulbs were at the apex of that ceiling, about forty feet up, and when one needed to be replaced, someone had to climb up a ladder and replace it. The ladder I used stretched out to be about thirty or forty feet tall. While someone held the base of the ladder, I fearlessly and quickly climbed to the top rungs to replace light bulbs. Had I fallen I would have landed on wooden pews and could have killed myself or been paralyzed for life. I didn't even think about the possibility of falling. As I think back on those days, I realize that I didn't have a healthy respect for the risks of ministry situations. Had I analyzed the risks better, I still would have climbed the ladder, but I would have done it much more carefully. In those days, I was moving ahead at full speed, not only in climbing tall ladders, but in ministry in general. There is a time to reflect on what is happening in our lives and ministries, and in my early years, I did very little reflection.

The lesson I learned from that first ladder experience was servanthood. The lesson of the second ladder was the value of deliberation, of weighing what we are doing and how we are doing it. Both of these lessons will come through loud and clear in this book. This book calls young leaders to seriously consider the major challenges they will face in the early years of ministry. The primary perspective that I encourage young leaders to take toward these challenges is that of a servant.

Young ministers are those between the ages of twenty and thirty or so. I was one of them back in those days, and I had a great introduction to the ministry. I worked with some great senior leaders, congregations, and colleagues. I have now been in full-time ministry for thirty-two years, and those early years were a good foundation for the subsequent years.

Today, I spend most of my time coaching and teaching Christian leaders, in the USA and overseas, through my ministry, Leadership Development Ministries. I've had the privilege of coaching ministers of all ages. The youngest was twenty-three and the oldest was sixty-three.

Several years ago, through my coaching, I began to see trends. I realized that ministers of the same age were facing similar kinds of challenges. For example, those in their twenties were facing similar challenges, but they were different from the challenges of those in their fifties. I thought it would be worthwhile to clarify the challenges ministers face in the same decade of life. Doing so might help me help many of them prepare for and overcome those challenges.

So I began my research. Initially, I thought about all of the young leaders I had coached, and then I tried to categorize the kinds of challenges they were facing. Then I extended my study by interviewing other young ministers. After that, I asked a number of ministers who were age thirty and older what kinds of challenges they had faced as they started out in ministry. And, finally, I reflected on my own challenges as I started out in ministry thirty years before.

As I continued on my research journey, I became convinced that this information would be helpful to a variety of ministers. It would help young ministers who were just starting out in ministry. It would also help coaches, mentors, and others who provide counsel to the young ministers.

Take a minute and ask yourself the same primary questions I asked in my interviews:

+ If you are between the ages of twenty and thirty and in full-time ministry, what are the challenges you are facing right now?

+ If you are older than thirty or so, think back to your earliest years in ministry: What challenges did you face as you began ministry?

+ And, if they were to ask you, what advice would you give to those young ministers just starting out in ministry?

Those were the questions that guided my research.

As you read this book you will find quotes from a variety of ministers. You will note that these challenges come right from the thoughts of young ministers themselves in some cases, and in other cases from the thoughts of older ministers as they reflect on their early years.

Contributors

After I finished my original research for this book, I asked two other leaders to contribute to it, too. I work with a variety of ministers, from young ones to older ones, but the other two contributors work with young ministers every day. Drew Smithson is the Southern California District Youth Director for the Assemblies of God. Mike DeVito is the Southwest Regional Director for the National Network of Youth Ministries. Both Drew and Mike train and coach young ministers and have been doing so for over 25 years.

We started meeting together every month about a year ago. I showed them what I had discovered about the challenges of young ministers, and we discussed those challenges together. I expected that they would have a wealth of knowledge to share. And I was right. Though we did not always agree, the discussions we had together were vital in the shaping of this book. Though I write in the first person, I would be remiss if I didn't acknowledge that Drew and Mike made valuable contributions to this book.

Laying a Good Foundation

If you are a young minister, either preparing for ministry, or in the early stages of your ministry, this book will help you understand the common challenges that young ministers face. I not only cite the challenges but I provide principles for dealing with those challenges. By reading this book you will be laying a good foundation of understanding that will help to carry through to success in your first few years of ministry.

Individual Challenges for Young Ministers

Challenge # 1

Solidifying Your Call to Full-time Ministry

More times than I would care to admit, I have started an exercise program only to abandon it when life's details or my schedule "forced out" the exercise program. I've learned that to stay on task, I really have to plan ahead and contend for the exercise program.

Starting out in full-time ministry is similar to that. It is one thing to feel called to full-time ministry when you are young and have no experience. It is another to follow through on that call to ministry once you begin to experience the challenges of ministry.

Young people who obey the call of God into full-time ministry often find that as they go through their twenties their call to ministry is tested. Some decide that full-time ministry is not for them and they drop out. For many others, the decade between ages twenty and thirty is a time of solidifying the call to full-time ministry.

There must be a commitment to the ministry. We are not in it for the money or the praise. Whatever your situation may be at the moment, whether good or bad, remember that God has called you. Many days things don't work out. You must endure them.

What exactly is the challenge?

1

Coming to Grips with the Call of God

I believe that all Christians are called to exercise their spiritual gifts, either in their local church or in some kind of ministry. They may be construction workers or doctors, but they are also called to further the kingdom of God in some way. I also believe that God continues to call some Christians to full-time ministry, i.e., to earn their income through their ministry. In Acts 13:2, we see many worshiping the Lord, but the Holy Spirit said, "Set apart for me Barnabas and Saul for the work to which I have called them." The Lord still calls people to full-time ministry and sets them apart.

The challenge is that young ministers may see the ministry as a chosen profession rather than a call from God. One difference between seeing your work as a chosen profession or as a call from God is how you view your options.

Everyone enters an occupation with incomplete information. The college graduate who decides to be an accountant has an incomplete view of what being an accountant is all about. The same is true for the people planning to be bellboys, businessman, or barristers. You just never know how much you will like your work, until you actually start doing it. After practicing your new occupation for a year you may be affirmed in it; or, you may suspect you made an incorrect choice. You simply may not like your work. That is why there is always a certain amount of attrition in every occupation. It is a fact of life.

Those who do not profess a supernatural calling to full-time ministry—be they accountants, construction workers, nurses, or whatever—can simply decide to change their occupations. But for those who sense a calling from God, the issue of obedience to God enters the picture. Ministers must be obedient to that calling.

One of the challenges in early, full-time ministry is how young ministers view their "calling." A denominational district supervisor put it this way:

> I have seen some leave the ministry, particularly during the first five years of ministry, whom I believe never came to grips with the call of God. I believe some of these have gone into the ministry as a vocation and not as a

call. They've chosen the ministry because they have a particular perception of a lifestyle. Upon discovering that the lifestyle was not equal to their expectations, they became disillusioned and left the ministry. Sometimes the disillusionment comes from broken relationships with members of a church staff or difficulty in relationships with people in the congregation. So the fallout I would attribute to not fully understanding what the call of God means.[1]

I would never judge a minister who leaves the ministry. That is not my job. The Scriptures tell us that the workman is accountable to his boss, and that is not me. I have been tempted to quit the ministry because of the financial and time requirements of our two special-needs children. I understand how life's many challenges can cause us to look at other options. Though there are exceptions that only God can rightly judge, it is generally true that a call to ministry is non-amendable.

Many leaders agree; they see their ministry as not optional. They have dedicated their lives to preaching the gospel and believe that there is no other option for them. Leaving the ministry has never been considered. They do what they do because God called them to do it.

A denominational district supervisor echoed this outlook:

Since I was about fifteen or sixteen, I knew that God had called me. It was a lifelong assignment from God himself that was non-amendable, non-negotiable. It was a mandate kind of thing with me. When the going gets tough, I say, "Man, this is some kind of a job I got," but I never question the call. I just know there is nothing else I'm supposed to do. Without a clear call to the pastorate, you don't have a chance of survival.[2]

That last line caught my attention the first time I read it. Though the call may occasionally seem like a straightjacket, it can also be our salvation. Our very survival in ministry may depend upon viewing our call as non-amendable and non-negotiable, just as the district supervisor above said.

Who hasn't wanted to quit the ministry? A pastor friend of mine says that pastors should never resign on Monday. He says they should think about it for a few days, reasoning that some Sundays are so difficult that it is easy to resign the following day. But when you have a call, you stay put, and usually you are glad you did later on. After being in full-time ministry for thirty-two years, I'm glad I've persevered. The main reason I have is that I have viewed my work as a calling, not a chosen profession.

Fulfilling the Call to Full-time Ministry Often Requires Sacrifice

If you are a young minister and you have entered into full-time ministry, you are probably not surprised to find that salaries in the ministry are meager. You were probably aware of that long before you took your first ministry position. However, the challenge is to deal with the salary issue over the long haul. It is one thing to be satisfied with your salary when things are going well in your ministry. It is another thing to be satisfied when your ministry circumstances are difficult, or when you are facing opposition in your church or ministry. To endure in ministry the minister must be willing to sacrifice.

Listen to the way one former youth minister expressed this sacrifice:

> When I was in college, I was told there would be discouraging times in ministry—and I knew I could handle discouragement—but I didn't think it would be this intense. I was ready to throw in the towel, I questioned my calling, my abilities, my spirituality (not to mention the spirituality of the church), and much more. Among my thoughts were, "I could make so much more money in a job that could be as fulfilling and less discouraging." My friend listened to my plight—and had a simple response, "God has called you and equipped you for ministry—stay there!" he said. After twenty-five years, I understand and deal with discouragement a little bit better—and I also make my living listening to youth pastors who feel the same emotions.[3]

4

The apostle Paul certainly faced tough financial times. He wrote, "Our hearts ache, but we always have joy. We are poor, but we give spiritual riches to others. We own nothing, and yet we have everything" (2 Cor. 6:10, NLT).

Like Paul, those in the ministry today often experience their own financial challenges. I have a minister friend who, in his first youth pastor position, worked five jobs to make ends meet. Spare time was hard to come by. He acknowledged that his schedule took a toll on his health. And then, in his second church, he had to live in government housing because he and his wife had so little money.

When I first began coaching ministers, there was a peculiar fear lurking in my heart. I knew that those I would be coaching would be opening their lives to me. Some would be sharing things with me that they normally don't share with anyone. As I reflected on that, I feared that I would lose respect for ministers because of what I would learn. It was a strange fear. I didn't take time to try to discern why I had this fear, but I specifically remember thinking about it. Well, after coaching many ministers of all ages for many years, I'm relieved that I can report that I continue to have great respect for them. I wouldn't dare to tell you they are perfect. We all know better. But I have seen behind the curtain and what I have seen brings much more hope than despair. Over the years, as ministers have described their challenges, I have been reminded time and time again that they are not in ministry for the money or the praise. I see their motives. Whatever their situation at the moment, whether good or bad, I'm inspired as I hear them remind themselves and me that God has called them, and that they will be true to their calling, regardless of suffering.

Paul wrote to young Timothy about suffering: "We work hard and suffer much in order that people will believe the truth..." (1 Tim. 4:10, NLT).

Consider the experience of an older minister as he describes his pre-full-time ministry years, and then his years as a full-time minister:

> I was working a secular job, but I sensed that God was calling me to full-time ministry, so my wife and I sent out my résumé to churches. One day we received a call from a friend, Pastor Bob, who said, "I just became lead pastor of this church, and we can't pay you, but we could use you on

staff. Interested?" We checked it out and finally decided to leave our city and move to his area. We went there as interns. Interestingly, right after I said yes to Bob I received a call about a very good secular job in my field of music. They offered a salary of forty thousand dollars a year. [Remember that he had signed on as a non-paid intern at the church]. And a voice said, "Are you sure you are called?" But I was, and I stayed on as intern at the church.

That man is now a lead pastor and has been in full-time ministry for about fifteen years. He had an opportunity to leave the ministry and work a secular job for a higher salary (in his case, an actual salary), but he chose to sacrifice and stay in ministry.

A youth director who has counseled many youth pastors explained to me what he has seen several times. He said that many young guys come out of college with a large student loan debt and they take youth pastor jobs with very meager salaries. Many of the youth pastors' friends are in fields such as the Information Technology sector, where they are earning 50 percent more or even double the salary of their old college buddies who are now youth pastors. Some youth pastors see this and decide to leave the ministry with the intention of temporarily taking a different job that pays more, paying off their debts, and then returning to full-time ministry. But, the youth director recollects, once they've paid off the debts, many do not return to full-time ministry.

Years ago I was speaking with Wesley Hurst, a former missionary director in Asia Pacific. He said that if people are called to be foreign missionaries, they should follow through on that call as soon as possible. I asked him, "Why the urgency?" He replied that he had known a number of people who professed a call to missions as young adults, but decided to wait until later in life to follow through on that call. The problem, Wesley explained, is that many get accustomed to a comfortable lifestyle in the USA and never actually make it to the foreign mission field.

When asked what advice he would give to people who are just starting out in ministry, one sixty-year-old minister said, "Be willing to start from the bottom. Paul worked with his hands. Much of my success had to do with the first three years of my ministry. I worked for those three years without being paid. I worked for nothing. That gave me a mindset."

I've known this minister for years, and I would judge him to have been very successful in ministry. Today, he lives in a nice house in a pricey neighborhood. Apparently, he didn't stay poor forever.

The sacrifice that ministers must make is not only financial, but also in esteem. One minister said that one reason pastors leave the ministry is what he calls "unrewarded vocation." He defined this as living in a culture where people have little respect for the ministry. In such a culture, ministers sacrifice not only financially, but also in esteem. They don't receive the same respect that ministers received in the past. He warned, "I think some are ill prepared for that."[4]

If you ask older ministers if they think that there has been a lessening of ministers' esteem in the eyes of others, they will say "yes." Many can recall times past when they were given discounts on train routes and golf course green fees simply because of the respect that society awarded ministers. In the past, American society respected ministers more than today. Of course, this lessening of respect applies to a number of institutions today, not just the ministry. For some, this lack of esteem for the ministry creates an obstacle to their continuing in ministry.

The Element of Risk

Are you willing to take risks in ministry? It is easy to settle for the comfortable, for the tried and true, for those positions that have a measure of security. But God does not seem to be as concerned as we do with making us comfortable. God called Abraham to an uncertain journey. Moses was called to lead murmuring wanderers. David had to wander in caves for a period of his life, and that was after he was aware of his calling to be king of Israel. The early disciples continued to follow Jesus Christ though they knew it was risky, and most of them paid dearly for that choice. The person who is looking for comfort and security may not find them in full-time ministry.

One older minister who now is in a ministry position that most would see as very successful, said this about risk: "I'm here today because of a willingness to take risks, and a wife who is willing to take risks too. God opened up opportunities for us, and each one was a risk. I'm thankful for the opportunities, even though we moved about every five years."

I'm talking about risks in ministry, but what are the specific risks in ministry? In ministry we aren't asked to take the Evel Knievel or movie-stunt-guy kind of risks. We are not asked to invest huge sums of money like capital investors. In the USA we are not asked to give our very lives for the gospel, as is the case in some repressive countries. So what kind of risks am I referring to?

I mention the two examples below with the "risk" of sounding like the father who tells his kids his story of having to walk ten miles in the cold, blowing snow to get to school. But, since this is a candid book that wants to treat honestly the challenges for young ministers, I'll take that "risk."

One risk for young ministers has to do with the planting of a church. One veteran minister reflected:

> I ask, "Are young ministers willing to take risks?" They want the car, and the nice house, and all the stuff... high standard of living. We were always willing to take risks. I don't think there are enough church entrepreneurs— those willing to go and plant a church. I see some, but I don't see a lot of them.

Another risk has to do more with a male minister's wife than the minister himself. A man who has been in ministry many years said this:

> [Risk] is that wife seeing herself as a partner, not just as having separate careers though they are married. Are wives willing to give up their career to follow their husbands' dreams? I know it is expensive to live today. It often takes two careers to make it. But my wife was willing to be a homemaker to follow my dream. There exists an unwillingness to take risks.

Those two quotes highlight two specific kinds of risks. I could list many more. One of the greatest risks was taken by Jesus when he left heaven and came to earth. Paul writes: "Though he was God, he did not demand and cling to his rights as God" (Philippians 2:6, NLT). The essence of risk in the kingdom of God is the surrender of our rights while clinging to God's will for our lives.

Fulfilling the Call Often Requires Resisting Pressure from Others

Those who are contemplating entering the ministry, or those who are young in the ministry, sometimes feel pressure from family members and much of that pressure originates from financial issues.

One twenty-five-year-old minister asserted that meager ministry salaries are the reason that parents and family members discourage guys like him from entering the ministry. He went on to say that their discouraging words are what cause him and other prospective ministers to doubt their self-worth and their ability to make ends meet in ministry.

Paul wrote to Timothy about being aware of the need to safeguard himself: "Keep a close watch on yourself and on your teaching. *Stay true to what is right,* and God will save you and those who hear you" (1 Tim. 4:16, NLT).

The call to ministry requires single-minded obedience to God. Others will have their opinions as to what a person should do, and their opinions are important, but the most important opinion is God's.

Jesus was pulled by those close to him to do certain things, but he stayed true to his calling. In John 7 we read that Jesus' brothers urged him to go to Judea, but Jesus said it was not the right time for such a visit. Jesus faced pressure from His family, too.

> *After this, Jesus stayed in Galilee, going from village to village. He wanted to stay out of Judea where the Jewish leaders were plotting his death. But soon it was time for the Festival of Shelters, and Jesus' brothers urged him to go to Judea for the celebration. "Go where your followers can see your miracles!" they scoffed. "You can't become a public figure if you hide like this! If you can do such wonderful things, prove it to the world!" For even his brothers didn't believe in him.*
>
> *Jesus replied, "Now is not the right time for me to go. But you can go anytime, and it will make no difference.* (John 7:1-6, NLT)

Resisting the pressure from those closest to us is difficult, but it may be necessary. They won't have to answer to God for your choices, but you will. Those close to you usually think that they have your best in mind. But I affirm what you already know, that doing God's will is what is most important.

Fulfilling the Call May Require an Entrepreneurial Spirit

Church networks and denominations differ greatly in the amount of support and networking they provide to young ministers who are looking to plug into a ministry position. In some denominations job placement is centralized and you are appointed by a bishop or supervisor to serve at a specific local church or ministry position. In other denominations and networks, if you are looking for a ministry position, the most you will get is some good will and best wishes: "Well, we hope you find a position. Have a good day."

Young ministers must understand what it takes to succeed in their context. Some denominations provide a lot of support and networking opportunities for their ministers. Other denominations provide little of that.

In one church network, the Assemblies of God (A/G), all ministers, including young ones, are expected to be entrepreneurial. Consider what one district superintendent had to say:

> The Assemblies of God, we really are kind of Darwinian, if that's a word. It's sort of survival of the fittest. But that's not all bad! And our young people coming out of our schools need to be taught, "Look there's no freebie in this whole thing. All you're going to have is an opportunity, and you're going to have to be very entrepreneurial." [5]

Another A/G district superintendent agreed:

> Any pastor who succeeds, I believe, must have an entrepreneurial approach to his life and ministry. Some come into the ministry because they think it's going to be easy to find a place to minister, and they fail to realize that every minister is a freelance operator. He's got to find his

own place in our constituency. Nobody appoints him to a pastorate. Some, lacking the entrepreneurial aspect of life, weary in their attempt to find a fulfilling pastorate.[6]

The key in this discussion is to understand what we must be and do to fulfill our God-given call in our specific ministry context. We are not called to be entrepreneurial just to be entrepreneurial. Our goal is to be obedient to God, and that may require an entrepreneurial attitude toward ministry in our context.

Jesus said to His disciples, "I will make you fishers of men." God has the ability to "make us" into something we are not naturally. If you are not naturally an entrepreneur, God will give you the grace to do what is necessary to fulfill His call in your life. This does not mean that He wants to make you into a used-car- salesman type of person. He does not want to make you pushy. But He may push you toward having more of an entrepreneurial spirit, and as you cooperate with Him you will find that God will empower you as you move forward.

Questions for Young Leaders

1. In what ways was your call to ministry similar to God's call to Paul and Barnabas, seen in Acts 13? In what ways was your call to ministry different from theirs?

2. What are the factors that reinforce and intensify your call to ministry? What are the factors that tend to undermine your call to ministry?

3. What are the risks inherent in your call to ministry?

4. How much of an entrepreneurial spirit is expected or required in your ministry context?

Questions for Lead Pastors or Ministry Directors

1. How has your view of God's call into full-time ministry changed over the years?

2. What can you do to nourish God's call in the lives of the young leaders who work with you?

3. What risks have you taken to fulfill God's call in your life?

Recommendations for Lead Pastors or Ministry Directors

1. Take 30 minutes at the end of a staff meeting to discuss God's call, challenges to the call, and risks inherent in the call.

2. Invite the young leaders you work with to stop by your office and discuss one-to-one God's call in their lives.

3. Initiate a discussion on the following question: How does our church network (denomination, fellowship, etc.) help or hinder you in your quest to follow God's call on your life?

4. Preach or lead a devotional on the subject of God's call into full-time ministry.

Challenge # 2

Knowing Yourself

One minister thought back to his early days of ministry and commented,

> When you are young and in ministry, you are identifying your identity. 'Who am I?' is a central question. And, 'What is my identity?' Before, it was easy, you were a student—you went to class and did the requirements and tried to be good at it. But then you enter the ministry and need to figure out who you are.

Knowing God and his ways—that is most important! But knowing yourself, your spiritual gifts, your natural abilities, your personality tendencies, your conflict-management style, and a host of other self-related issues—these are important, too.

One of the challenges for young ministers is the lack of self-knowledge. It can be frustrating. People tell us that as we look for work we should be guided by our strengths, passions, and giftings, but we really don't know ourselves very well. Our self-knowledge is limited—we can't quite figure out what is the best kind of job setting for us. We have hunches, and sometimes educated hunches, but it takes some experience to really know yourself.

Why is this self-knowledge important?

Knowing Who You Are Provides Direction

Early in his ministry, Pastor Steve Bierly met with a wise old pastor who told him that he was going to tell Steve his most important task in his first five years as a pastor. Steve expected the message to be "keep daily devotions" or "run annual stewardship campaigns" or some other similar message. Instead the wise man said, "The most important thing you'll do in the first five years is to discover who Steve Bierly is as a pastor."[7] You must understand your gifts and passions. If you do not, you will try to fulfill others' expectations instead of focusing on God's plan for you.

The Scriptures Instruct Us to Know Our Gifts

The Scriptures tell us to understand our spiritual gifts. The Scriptures assume that we will know our gifts, and that we should use our gifts appropriately.

> *God has given each of us the ability to do certain things well. So if God has given you the ability to prophesy, speak out when you have faith that God is speaking through you. If your gift is that of serving others, serve them well. If you are a teacher, do a good job of teaching. If your gift is to encourage others, do it! If you have money, share it generously. If God has given you leadership ability, take the responsibility seriously. And if you have a gift for showing kindness to others, do it gladly.* (Romans 12:6-8, NLT)

Knowing Yourself Includes Emotional Self-Awareness

Knowing yourself involves not only your gifts and talents, but also your emotions. We need to be emotionally self-aware. When we are not aware of our emotions they can control our actions and thoughts. Have you ever seen someone who is at the mercy of his emotions? Years ago I was waiting in line at the Garuda Airlines ticket counter at the Jakarta, Indonesia airport. Just in front of me was a middle-age Australian man and, as his turn came and he stepped to the counter, I heard the ticket agent inform him that he was too late to catch his plane to Singapore, and that he would need to find a hotel and wait until the following day for the next flight to Singapore. Hearing this, the man became angry. At first, he just complained about the airline service, but then he began yelling at the agent, calling her and the airline some choice names. She countered that there was nothing she could do. Then, to my astonishment, he picked up his suitcase and threw it at her. Fortunately, she stepped back and it barely landed on her toes. Now there was a man whose emotions had hijacked his person. In the ministry we may not react so violently to people in our ministries (hopefully), but we must be aware of how our emotional state is affecting who we are and what we're doing.

Only when we understand our emotions can we manage them. And, when we manage them, we improve our chances of developing positive relationships with others. Think of it this way: Being aware of our emotions enables us to manage our emotions, and that helps us build positive relationships.

I was speaking with a lead pastor about the challenges facing his staff members, and, after reflecting for a few minutes, he linked a lack of gentleness to a lack of emotional awareness. From his perspective, what suffers most when we are not aware of our emotional state is our ability to be gentle with others. Gentleness, of course, is of paramount importance for ministers. Paul lists gentleness as a fruit of the Spirit in Galatians 5. He instructs Timothy to gently instruct others. This pastor warned, "Leaders need to be careful not to react out of their own issues." What does it mean to react out of our own issues? It means that we project our emotional state onto others. A common way is that we get hurt and then react to others out of our hurt or anger. We get easily irritated with others. We treat people in an abrasive way without realizing the impact we're having. This pastor had seen staff members react out of their own issues and he concluded that when they do so, it hurts their ability to be gentle with people.

Emotional self-awareness is something that ministers of all ages should learn, but it's important early on to grasp the value of this self-awareness.

Dealing with Your Own Insecurities

Is anyone above the need to deal with his or her own insecurities? I think all ministers, young and old, face a certain amount of insecurity. You'll have those moments when you're face to face with your insecurities. You may ask, "Can I do this job?" "Do I have what it takes?" "What about that other guy (or gal) who I sort of see as my competitor—how do I compare with him (or her)?" These are normal questions for ministers. The important thing is to acknowledge (to ourselves) our insecurities and commit them to God, asking Him for His help. Too often we deny our insecurities, and then never allow God to deal with them.

Helen Musick was a young youth pastor who wanted to connect with the young people in her youth group. One goal she had was to get in touch with each of the young people in her youth group, so she decided to call each one. But she felt very shy and insecure about talking to them, even on the phone, because of their unpredictability. She had this to say about the effect her own insecurities had on her attempts at talks with young people:

> Teenagers are often unpredictable, inconsistent, and not easily decoded. I learned that early on as I undertook relationship building. And the old saying, "If at first you don't succeed, try, try again" bears repeating when you're trying to establish regular communication with students. For some of us, conversation and interaction come easily. But for many of us, the lurking voices of insecurity drive us from reaching out the way we really want to. It's during these moments that we must remember, "In our weakness, his strength is made perfect." And then our insecurity becomes our greatest gift, because it pushes us toward deeper dependence on Jesus.[8]

Helen hit the nail on the head. Our dependence must be on Christ.

I learned to give my insecurities to Christ and depend on Him during the first Bible school class I taught in the French language. In 1988, my wife, Sherie, and I had just finished studying French in Paris when we went as missionaries to French Polynesia, a group of islands in the South Pacific. I was scheduled to teach a class at our Bible school there, but I was extremely insecure about my ability to teach in French. It helped to write out all my notes in advance so that, if I needed to, I could simply read them. But I was insecure about the questions the students might ask: Would I be able to understand their questions? What if they had an accent and I couldn't understand what they were asking? That would be embarrassing to me and to them. What if I didn't know the proper theological terms?

All of these questions caused me to be fearful. In fact, I was so fearful that about two hours before the first classroom session I laid down for a fifteen-minute nap and found that I could hardly move—I was paralyzed by fear. I finally responded to the fear by committing myself to teach, and to depend on Christ for His help. Then I forced myself to get up from the nap, go to the school, and get started. I taught the class that day and many other classes in the subsequent months, and I enjoyed teaching each one.

I think that one key to handling our insecurities is found in a Scriptural statement related to belief. The New Testament words, "I do believe, but help me not to doubt" (Mark 9:24, NLT) were an acknowledgement of faith, but also a plea to the Lord for help. That's a great way to handle our insecurities, saying to the Lord, "I'm acknowledging this insecurity in my life, and I confess my faith in you for this area of my life, but, Lord, help me!" Helen Musick acknowledged her shyness about reaching out to young people, and I acknowledged my fears about teaching in French, but then we both moved forward in dependence on Christ. In other words, you are not denying that you need God's help with the insecurity. You are acknowledging that you have a battle on your hands, but you're also acknowledging that through Christ you will overcome. Then you move forward in faith.

Maintaining Our Focus

One ministry challenge is maintaining our focus on God as we experience our own trials. Have you noticed that the challenges of life and ministry can make you drift away from being God-focused and others-focused, to being self-focused? Sometimes the challenges we face seem so overwhelming that we become discouraged, and then we find it difficult to help others. In those situations our self-focus can cloud our faith in God and concern for others.

I'm amazed at the Apostle Paul's selflessness, at his focus on others. Consider the book of Philippians that Paul wrote while he was in prison. In spite of his chains his focus remained on the Philippians. With all the challenges he was facing he could have chosen to focus on his own problems, but he didn't. In the first 8 verses he uses the word, "you" ten times (NLT). In Philippians 1:8, Paul writes, *"God knows how much I love you and long for you with the tender compassion of Christ Jesus."* In spite of his many challenges he remained focused on helping others.

If you are a youth pastor, you minister to young people who are facing the crises that often occur during the teenage years. Teenagers get rejected in romantic relationships, rebel against authority, and experience emotional highs and lows. Whatever the crisis experienced by the young people, the young leader ministering to them, whatever his own challenges, must be able to focus on the young people in his care. Teenagers need people of stability and wisdom around them during those difficult years.

In my years of coaching leaders, God has enabled me to handle my own challenges so that I've been able to focus entirely on the leaders during our meetings. But there was one exception. I remember it well. I was going through a particularly difficult challenge and I was very discouraged. When I arrived at the pastor's office to coach him, to my dismay, he noticed the discouragement in my countenance. I decided to share with him the challenge I was facing. Immediately, he focused on me and he prayed for me, then we continued our coaching meeting. But somehow, in a way I still don't fully understand, that initial exchange weakened my coaching effectiveness that day. I'm of the opinion that when the coach is transparent in coaching relationships, it actually helps the leader being coached to feel a link with the coach. But in this situation on that day, instead of my challenges creating a connection to the leader I was coaching, it actually was an obstacle to our communication.

Often, sharing our discouraging challenges with those we are ministering to creates a bond with them. But this works best when we do so with a sense of peace and faith in our own heart.

Paul wrote to young Timothy about not losing his focus:

> *Again I say, don't get involved in foolish, ignorant arguments that only start fights. The Lord's servants must not quarrel but must be kind to everyone. They must be able to teach effectively and be patient with difficult people. They should gently teach those who oppose the truth...* (2 Tim. 2:23-25, NLT)

Paul uses such terms as "don't get involved in..." (v. 23), "must not..." (v. 24), and "must be able to..." to describe the self-control that was needed in order for Timothy to be an effective leader.

Later, in that same letter, Paul tells Timothy to keep his poise: *But you should keep a clear mind in every situation.… Complete the ministry God has given you.* (2 Tim. 4:5, NLT)

Young ministers must learn to trust the strength of the Lord in their lives, and then focus on the people God has given to them for ministry.

Search Out the Affirmers

As you deal with your own insecurities look for others who will build you up. Affirming words strengthen us. Someone said, "I can live a week on one compliment."

You eat nutritious food to maintain your health. You exercise to build strong muscles. You think good thoughts to develop good habits. Why not spend time each week with an encourager to strengthen your emotional and spiritual health? Affirmers are out there. Find them and enjoy how God works through them. You need them!

A lead pastor talked about his relationship with his church staff:

> Confidence is a huge deal for young ministers. I try to provide as much affirmation as possible for guys in my church. I communicate strongly that "you will be much better in ministry than me," and "you will do well." I want to build them up. There are so many insecure people out there in ministry. We need affirmation; therefore we are drawn toward people who offer it.

That pastor offered affirmation to those on his staff. But sometimes you've got to look outside your immediate context for affirmation. After I wrote an early draft of this book, I sent it to a few friends and asked them to critique it. One friend responded to this point about the need for affirmation and stated that early in their ministry, she and her husband had to look outside their immediate context for affirmation. Her quote was so true-to-life that I decided I had to include it here.

> This is a really good point and could be elaborated much more. What if you're in a small church? Our first staff positions were in a church that really disliked the lead pastor, and the congregation was very hard on us because

we stayed loyal to him. After such a positive environment in our Christian university, it was shocking and hurtful to be so criticized. We had to go outside our church and find friends on staff at another church to "repair" our bruised egos. Also, what if your lead pastor is part of the problem? We experienced that at our second church. I think pain and disillusionment with ministry and church people are perhaps one of the hardest things about starting out in ministry.

Just like this couple, you may have to go outside your immediate setting to find affirmers. The effort will be worth it.

Understand How You Deal with Conflict

One area of our personality that we should try to understand is our conflict management style. In the research I completed for my book *Pressing On! Why Leaders Derail and What To Do About It*, I found eleven major reasons that leaders derail from ministry.

Derailment Factors
+ Inability to resolve conflicts
+ Character fault(s)
+ Burn-out
+ Inability to adapt or develop
+ Lack of accountability
+ Bitterness
+ Inability to build and lead a team of workers and/or staff
+ Lack of financial integrity
+ Inability to deal with the expectations placed upon the leader
+ Spiritual doubt, loss of confidence in God and His faithfulness
+ Self-doubt, lack of self-confidence[9]

These factors are significant not just in the USA. In my workshops I've cited these factors to leaders in more than ten countries, and all of those leaders confirmed that in their country, one of the major reasons that Christian leaders derail is the inability to resolve conflict. Sadly, too many leaders, particularly young ministers, have never taken the time to understand how they normally handle conflict.

One minister found it enlightening to take time to reflect on, and be honest about, his conflict style. He related that after about ten years in ministry, he realized that whenever conflict had arisen in his pastoral ministry, he simply moved on to another church. In ten years he had been pastor of three churches. In his first church a conflict situation arose, and rather than deal with the conflict, he resigned and moved on to another. In another church, a difficult conflict occurred in year five, but at that point he again resigned and moved on to another church. After some reflection, he realized that his conflict style was to avoid conflict. He concluded that if he didn't change his conflict style, he would probably continue his habit of leaving churches whenever major conflicts occurred, and he might have quite a long string of short pastorates.

What Is Your Conflict Management Style?
The five common conflict management styles are:

A. Avoidance Style
   Objective: Avoid having to deal with conflict.
   The intent of this style is to *stay out* of the conflict, to avoid being identified with either side.

B. Accommodation Style
   Objective: Don't upset the other person.
   The intent of this style is to *preserve* the relationship at all costs.

C. Collaboration Style
   Objective: Solve the problem together.
   The intent of this style is to get all the parties *fully involved* in defining the conflict and in carrying out mutually agreeable steps for managing the conflict.

D. Compromise Style
   Objective: You want to reach an agreement quickly.

The intent of this style is to provide each side with a small win in order to persuade each to accept a loss.

E. Competition Style
Objective: You want to get your way.
The intent of this style is to *win*.

Take a moment and reflect on your experiences in life and ministry, asking, "Which of these styles do I normally practice when I face a conflict?"

Family Conflict Styles:
Take a few minutes to think of how conflict was handled in your family. What were your parents' conflict styles?

Father: _____ conflict management style
Mother: _____ conflict management style

What lessons can you learn from conflicts in your family as you grew up?

What conflict lessons did you learn from parents?

What conflict lessons did you learn from siblings?

What conflict lessons did you learn from your own experiences while growing up?

This is only a cursory treatment of understanding your conflict style. I would recommend you take a conflict-management inventory, and that you also ask some friends to assess your style.

Questions for Young Leaders

1. How would you rate your grasp of your identity? (Choose one)
    + Excellent understanding
    + Good understanding
    + Some understanding
    + Little understanding

2. What are your...
   + spiritual gifts?
   + strengths?
   + personality tendencies?
   + conflict-management styles or style?
   + passions?

3. Your understanding of who you are and what you can do has probably steered you into your present work position. How is the fit between who you are and your present position? How does your work suit you (or not suit you)?

4. What insecurities do you have in regard to your identity and your work?

5. Who are the people who affirm you?

Questions for Lead Pastors or Ministry Directors

1. How could you help the young leaders who work with you understand their identity?

2. What could you do in staff meetings to affirm your young ministers? What methods, role plays, or exercises could you utilize to affirm them? Here is a quick one: Make a list of twenty positive adjectives (examples: empathetic, dependable) and then choose three that describe a young minister. Then, explain to the young minister how the adjectives describe him or her.

3. What have you learned about conflict in the ministry that you could pass on to young ministers?

Recommendations for Lead Pastors or Ministry Directors

1. Consider administering a 360-degree assessment to the young ministers who work with you. (In a 360-degree assessment the

young leader assesses himself or herself, and then others assess the young leader, too. These assessments provide a good picture of reality. Contact me at BenjaminMKaufman@cs.com to set up an assessment.)

2. Have each member of your staff complete a conflict-management inventory and discuss the results with each other.

Challenge # 3

Lack of Credibility

If you are a youth pastor, or if you were at one time a youth pastor, have you ever felt like this guy? "I was discouraged because no matter how hard I tried, parents still saw me as a baby-sitter for their teenagers."[10]

One of the challenges you may face as a young minister is a lack of respect from others older than you. That lack of respect has resulted in names that are given to young ministers and generally to all young workers: rookie, greenie, the new guy on the block, neophyte, and naïve one. And those are only the relatively kind names.

Similar situations occur in the other areas of life. In college, the freshmen are hazed to initiate them to life in the dorm or fraternity. Similarly, in a business, the new, young worker is often expected to do the jobs no one else wants. When the young, new guy offers his opinion it is common to hear, "What does he know? He's just a kid."

How does this play out in the ministry?

In the ministry, too, often others don't acknowledge the young leader's worth. In a church, for example, the young minister may not be perceived as a real pastor by the rest of the church staff. Yes, he is on staff, but he isn't offered the same esteem as the ministers on staff. He might be referred to as just the "rec" (recreation) guy.

Not only does this happen within a church staff, but young ministers in a church may sense this same lack of esteem from members of their congregation members. Congregation members might fail to show respect for the youth minister, for example, because they didn't hire him; the lead pastor did. Many within large congregations don't even know the name of their youth pastor and other assistant pastors.

Often, in addition to this lack of respect from congregation members, the young leader lacks self-confidence. I met with a group of college students who were preparing for the ministry and asked them to cite the greatest challenge they were facing. Several responded that they didn't feel they had anything important to say or contribute in a church or ministry. As one young and aspiring minister said, "I haven't proven anything."

I advise young ministers to avoid one of two extremes: The first is that they know it all and that older folks should get out of the way so that something can be accomplished. You can guess how well that is received. I find few "rookie" ministers with that attitude. The other extreme to avoid is feeling that you, as a young minister, have nothing to say or contribute. That attitude should be cause for concern for all of us, because ministries need the creative, cutting-edge ideas of young ministers.

Earning Credibility

Years ago the main message of an investment firm's popular TV commercial was, "We get money the old fashioned way, we earn it." I haven't seen that commercial for years, so the words may not be exact, but I remember that message. I would like to borrow that message and translate it to the ministry: *Credibility must be earned.*

I'm writing primarily to young ministers, and most of you were not born prior to the 1980s. Prior to about the 1980s, the trust ascribed to ministers in the USA was high. But somewhere along around the 1980s or so, ministers' credibility in the eyes of the public declined. Perhaps it had to do with some high-profile televangelist scandals that occurred in the mid-1980s. Perhaps it was due to the general lessening of trust awarded to all institutions, including the church. But, somewhere along the line, the credibility of ministers in American society seems to have taken a tumble.

How much credibility do you have?
There are at least four core elements that form a person's credibility:

Core 1 – Integrity: Are you congruent?
A person of integrity is honest, has a reputation for being truthful, and will not lie.

Core 2 – Intent: What's your agenda?
A person of good intent doesn't try to deceive anyone, nor does he have hidden motives or agendas that would color his testimony.

Core 3 – Capabilities: Are you relevant?
A capable person has excellent credentials, expertise, knowledge, skill, and capability in the matter at hand.

Core 4 – Results: What's your track record?
If you have good results, you have a good track record, you have demonstrated your capabilities effectively in other situations in the past, you produce results, and there is a good reason to believe you will do so now.[11]

Those are some of the most important elements of credibility. Take a moment and rate yourself on each core. On a scale of 1 to 7, with 1 being the lowest and 7 the highest, how would you rate yourself on each of these core areas of credibility in your present job? For each core, circle one number between 1 and 7 to indicate where you see yourself. Be honest with yourself.

Core 1 – Integrity	1	2	3	4	5	6	7
Core 2 – Intent	1	2	3	4	5	6	7
Core 3 – Capabilities	1	2	3	4	5	6	7
Core 4 – Results	1	2	3	4	5	6	7

Take a look at your results, and ask the following questions:
+ In what areas can you improve your credibility?
+ What are the obstacles to improving?
+ What can you not improve? (For example, your past results cannot be changed.)
+ What questions are raised as a result of doing this exercise?
+ Would you benefit from asking a friend or colleague to rate you on these four core areas?

Building Credibility Takes Time

It takes time to build or improve one's credibility. It is important to accept this fact and take the long-term view. The longer you stay at your present job, and do a good job, the more credibility you will build.

Recently, I viewed the website of a nearby church and read about the resignation of their executive pastor. He was resigning to move overseas and be a missionary. I don't know this pastor, but judging by his website picture I guessed that he must be about forty or so. On the website he was saying "goodbye" to his church, and as part of his goodbye he explained that he had been raised in the church where he is now executive pastor. He then listed the various positions he had held over the years: youth group leader (as a teenager), youth group intern, youth pastor, associate pastor, and finally executive pastor. All in all, he had spent more than twenty years in an assistant position of some kind in that church.

I'd imagine that if we had the opportunity to talk with him we would find that now, after years of faithful service at that church, he has much greater credibility than he did twenty, or even ten years ago. It simply took time (matched with competence) to increase his credibility.

Fast-tracking your credibility. I have seen young leaders "fast track" their credibility by taking on and succeeding at major challenges early in their ministries. I know a former youth pastor who did this. Years ago, this young youth pastor successfully assumed the leadership of a summer, regional Christian concert that hosted about twenty music groups in several days of concerts. It was attended by thousands of young people, many of whom camped on the concert grounds. Handling all the logistics of such an event must have been quite a challenge. That "summer job" was in addition to his regular youth pastor duties. Apparently he did a great job. Others noticed his organizational ability and his credibility shot up. He "fast tracked" his credibility by taking on and succeeding at a particularly challenging job.

In contrast to "fast track" young leaders are those who lose credibility over the years. There are many reasons for this, all related in some way to one or more of the four credibility cores above.

Ministering at the church where you grew up: If you are ministering now at the church where you grew up, you will find that your past will either fast-track your credibility, or your past will hinder it. I interviewed a twenty-nine-year-old minister in this situation, who said the following: "People at our church remember me for my rebellious years. They don't see me differently today. But I'm not twelve anymore."

Ministers who are on staff at the church where they grew up may find that it takes longer to build credibility as a minister in the eyes of their congregation. Others may find that, as they start in their ministry positions, they already have a lot of credibility.

Whatever your level of credibility, ministering in the same church where you grew up presents not only some blessings, but some challenges. A lead pastor who has several associate pastors who grew up in the church, had this to say: "Among my associate pastors are those who grew up in this church.... Their families—nuclear and extended—are also in the church. So the question for my staff members is how to continue those friendships and family ties but maintain respect as a pastor."

Early in your ministry, try not to be anxious about your lack of credibility. It will come in time, assuming you are doing a good job. Notice the balance in the following two verses:

> "Give your complete attention to these matters. Throw yourself into your tasks so that everyone will see your progress. Keep a close watch on yourself and on your teaching. Stay true to what is right, and God will save you and those who hear you" (1 Tim. 4:15-16, NLT).

Verse 15 has the sense of surging forward and making great gains. Verse 16 sounds a note of caution—keep a close watch and stay true. There is wisdom in this balance. Some young leaders surge ahead with little thought that too much ambition can hurt you. Others are way too cautious—they should throw themselves more into their tasks.

Testing Precedes Authority

The Scriptures treat the credibility that comes with spiritual authority as a trust. We, as leaders, must earn that trust.

Paul writes to Timothy 1 Tim. 3:1-5 (NLT)

> It is a true saying that if someone wants to be an elder, he desires an honorable responsibility. For an elder must be a man whose life cannot be spoken against. He must be faithful to his wife. He must exhibit self-control, live wisely, and have a good reputation. He must enjoy having guests in his home and must be able to teach. He must not be a heavy drinker or be violent. He must be gentle, peace loving, and

> *not one who loves money. He must manage his own family*
> *well, with children who respect and obey him. For if a man*
> *cannot manage his own household, how can he take care of*
> *God's church?*

God does not permit just anyone to oversee his people. There are a bunch of "must be's" and "must not be's" in these verses. Verse 2 says, "Now the overseer must be…" Verse 6 says, "He must not be…"

And, in the same chapter, verses 8-10 affirm that deacons must earn their credibility. In 1 Tim. 3:10 we see these instructions: *"Before they are appointed as deacons, they should be given other responsibilities in the church as a test of their character and ability. If they do well, then they may serve as deacons."*

Verse 10, in particular, teaches the testing preceding authority principle, *"They must first be tested, and then if there is nothing against them, let them serve as deacons."*

A great example of one who proved his trustworthiness is Joseph. After Joseph was appointed to the second highest position in the Egyptian government, he wanted to return to Canaan to bury his father (Genesis 50:5). The disquieting question for Egypt's Pharaoh was this: After Joseph buried his father, would he return to Egypt? Apparently Pharaoh concluded that Joseph had been tested and had proven himself, because he allowed Joseph to return to Israel for a time.

The Life Application Bible had this to say about Joseph:

> Joseph had proven himself trustworthy as Pharaoh's
> adviser. Because of his good record, Pharaoh had little
> doubt that he would return to Egypt as promised
> after burying his father in Canaan. Privileges and
> freedom often result when we have demonstrated our
> trustworthiness. Since trust must be built gradually over
> time, take every opportunity to prove your reliability
> even in minor matters.[12]

I find it instructive that when Paul was writing to Timothy about his spiritual authority, he did not instruct Timothy to demand that others to listen to him simply due to his ministry position as spiritual overseer. Paul didn't say, "Tell the people who are in your church to obey you *because I placed you in charge there."* In other words, Paul did not say that Timothy's spiritual authority was based on his leadership position.

Instead, Paul writes the following to Timothy:

> *Teach these things and insist that everyone learn them. Don't let anyone think less of you because you are young. Be an example to all believers in what you teach, in the way you live, in your love, your faith, and your purity.* (1 Tim. 4:11-12)

Timothy's authority derives from his example, his very life. Paul tells Timothy that he should teach without apology and that he should insist that others learn—notice that there is no soft pedaling of Timothy's authority here, no reason for Timothy to be timid about teaching God's Word because he was young. But then Paul goes on to say that Timothy's spiritual authority should originate from his modeling of godliness. Once again, we see the idea that testing should come before authority is exercised.

Credibility and Educational Level

A common misconception among young ministers is that once they enter the work force on a full-time basis, others will ascribe a similar value to their education as they themselves do. Anyone who has just spent four or five years diligently studying in college naturally has the opinion expressed in this question: "Shouldn't all that work count for something?" And, of course, yes it should.

Our education is a part of our core credibility, but sometimes we overrate how much others will value it. Think of it, you've just spent countless hours studying and perhaps incurring a huge school debt. Then you graduate from college and begin working in a local church with a variety of people, some of whom have little respect for a college degree. You may be offended that others don't value your painstaking educational preparation as much as you do.

But, really, your education is just one part of the larger picture of credibility. In the four credibility cores above, it is part of the Capabilities Core (#3) that relates to expertise, knowledge, and skill. It is important, no question about that, but others may not value it as much as you do. This is one of those facts of life that you've got to accept and move on.

Your Credibility and Your Predecessors

Your credibility is assessed, to some degree, on the legacy of your predecessors. Some young leaders will inherit a measure of instant credibility because of their predecessor. Others will inherit a credibility liability due simply to the negative legacy of their predecessor or predecessors. All leaders must deal with the legacy, either positive or negative, of their predecessors.

What did you inherit when you took your present ministry position? How much credibility came with your position?

There are two categories to think of when considering the legacy of your predecessors:

First, there is the long-term credibility in your church that is associated with *all* your predecessors at your church or ministry. Second, there is the current credibility associated with the *most recent* predecessor in your church or ministry.

All your predecessors: The legacy of other young ministers over the years at your church or your ministry affects your credibility. If you had the information about all the young ministers who have ministered at your church over the years, would it show that they left a good or bad legacy? For example, if the church has had just three youth pastors in its twenty-five-year history and each has stayed at the church for about eight years, then you are probably inheriting a good legacy. That is exceptional stability and probably means that the congregation has a high level of trust in the position of "youth pastor." But if the church has had five youth pastors in the last eight years, that is a shaky legacy, and there is probably little trust in the youth pastor position. Sadly, the latter case is more common.

Your most recent predecessor: What is the legacy of the guy or gal you replaced? In your first weeks in a new ministry position, you can't do much about the credibility you inherited from your predecessor. Yes, you can assure the individuals in the congregation that you will do a much better job than your predecessor and they may give you the benefit of the doubt, but they really won't be convinced until they actually see a difference between you and your predecessor. It simply takes time to overcome a bad example.

But there is a flip side, a positive side, to this factor: If you follow someone who was a bad example you have the potential to turn things around and restore confidence in your ministry position. Your goal should not be to further your reputation at your predecessor's expense. But it is inevitable that others will compare you with your predecessor. So, if you are following what was a bad example, take the perspective that you have the opportunity to rebuild credibility. For example, if you are a youth pastor and your predecessor "left a bad taste" at your church, you should speak favorably (or just not at all) of your predecessor, and let your actions restore confidence in the position of youth pastor. Doing so will increase your credibility.

If you have the opposite situation and you are following a predecessor who oversaw great growth and was favorably viewed, see that as a great opportunity, too, and be grateful for your predecessor. The bar has been set high and the expectations toward you are high. You have inherited a high level of credibility.

Credibility among Peers

I didn't watch the TV series "Band of Brothers," but I really like that title. There is something fascinating about being part of a band of brothers that is moving forward with purpose to achieve some goal.

I've been part of a lot of teams through the years. I've been on basketball teams, football teams, church staff teams, missionary teams, and music teams, to name of few. The fun that I found in those activities was being part of a team, the camaraderie of working with other guys and gals.

I hope that you, as a young minister, find a welcoming team in your early church or ministry staff experiences. Through my conversations with young ministers I've discovered that many anticipate an inviting, kingdom-based team that values their contribution. But some have been shocked to find that some team members treated them with little respect simply because they were new and young. The young leaders expected camaraderie but found belittling. They expected a "band of brothers" (a warm team) but were disappointed.

A fifty-year-old minister reflected on his days as a youth pastor in the church where he is now lead pastor:

> One thing I hated when I was the youth pastor here, is
> that people and other associates would say, "You've got

to pay your dues." I determined that I would not say that to a youth pastor. I want him to feel like a regular and important part of the staff. I want our youth pastor to feel like part of the team.

Like this pastor, the apostle Paul treated his co-workers as integral members of his team. Paul had his "band of brothers." In 2 Timothy 4:9-13, toward the end of his life, he mentions some who were or had been part of his "band."

> *Please come as soon as you can. Demas has deserted me because he loves the things of this life and has gone to Thessalonica. Crescens has gone to Galatia, and Titus has gone to Dalmatia. Only Luke is with me. Bring Mark with you when you come, for he will be helpful to me. I sent Tychicus to Ephesus. When you come, be sure to bring the coat I left with Carpus at Troas. Also bring my books, and especially my papers.*

Paul mentions seven co-workers in this passage and he is writing to the eighth, Timothy. Obviously, he valued his team members and even felt betrayed when one, Demas, deserted him.

Paul's writings to Timothy demonstrate a kindhearted father-son kind of relationship. Listen to Paul's words to Timothy right at the opening of the book of 1 Timothy: *"Timothy, my son, here are my instructions for you, based on the prophetic words spoken about you earlier. May they give you the confidence to fight well in the Lord's battles"* (1 Tim 1:18).

Paul speaks to Timothy with warm words, as "my son." He reminds Timothy of an instructive prophetic experience earlier in his life. Paul encourages Timothy. Notice what Paul does not do: He does not call Timothy "the rookie," and remind him that he must "pay his dues," just as he, Paul, has done. He does not chide Timothy for being the new guy on the block.

Perhaps the reason Paul took such a kind approach to "the new guy on the block" is that he was conscious of the rigorous spiritual war in which he and Timothy were involved. Speaking of the prophetic words spoken over Timothy, Paul writes, "May they give you the confidence to fight well in the Lord's battles." Paul was aware that spiritual labor was not simply a game. It was serious business. Notice what Paul says in the very next verse: *"Cling tightly to your faith in Christ, and always keep your conscience clear. For some people have deliberately violated their consciences; as a result, their faith has been shipwrecked"* (1 Tim. 1:19). The eternal destiny of people, including Timothy, was at stake.

Paul was concerned for Timothy's own faith, for Timothy's own eternal destiny. Later, in his second letter to Timothy, Paul writes, *"Keep a close watch on yourself and on your teaching. Stay true to what is right, and God will save you and those who hear you* (1 Tim. 4:16).

These days, whenever I hear the phrase, "Keep a close watch on..." I think of children who should be guarded against molesters and kidnappers. Perhaps I've watched too many TV detective programs like "CSI" and "Criminal Minds" that often feature serial killers and child molesters. When we say "keep a close watch" in the context of our children, a deep emotion accompanies our action of watching. That emotion is intense; it causes us be particularly vigilant.

Paul uses those words, "keep a close watch," in a warmhearted way to express his concern and affection for Timothy. Paul is encouraging Timothy to "watch out" for his own faith, to guard it against what would destroy it. This is a different spirit from the one that exists when the new guy or gal on staff is treated with disrespect.

I've described Paul's warm relationship to Timothy and his other team members. I hope that you find these kinds of relationships in the ministry. But if you don't I hope that citing Paul's example will encourage you to treat those who work with you and under you as Paul treated Timothy.

When staff members treat each other with such respect, this does not mean that staff meetings and relationships should always be serious, without jesting or kidding. Actually, my experience is that when there is a spirit of love and respect among staff members it always seems to be accompanied by plenty of laughter and fun. That is as it should be!

One final note is important. I am not advocating that you, as perhaps the youngest and least experienced staff member, should be pampered or coddled. I know that you don't want that! And, the experienced staff members won't do that. As with any job there are real expectations toward anyone entering the ministry. The new guy or gal on the block is expected to do his or her job. Failure is possible. Being fired is possible. I cited Paul as an example of one who had a supportive, affectionate relationship with his team members. But we must not forget the story of Paul and John Mark. Paul and his team took young John Mark with them on Paul's second missionary journey, but John Mark deserted them. In other words, John Mark failed (Acts 13:5, 13). As a result of John Mark's desertion, Paul fiercely opposed Barnabas' suggestion to take John Mark with them on the next missionary journey (Acts 15:37, 38). From Paul's perspective, John Mark had failed and was not worthy of the position of missionary, at least not on Paul's team. Fortunately, with the help of Barnabas, Mark eventually proved himself and Paul later put him back on his team (2 Timothy 4:11).

John Mark's case bears out the reality that you as a young minister need other, older ministers who will come alongside you, lending you a hand, and helping you build the credibility you need to do well in ministry.

Questions for Young Leaders

1. What has hurt your credibility in the past?

2. What might hurt your credibility in the present?

3. What could you do to build your credibility?

4. In this chapter I cite four core elements of credibility (integrity, intent, capabilities, and results). I asked the follow-up question, "Would you benefit from asking a friend or colleague to rate you on these four core areas?"

   If the answer is yes, what friend or friends could you ask to rate you?

   Would you feel comfortable asking your boss to rate you? Would your boss feel comfortable rating you?

5. Consider those who held your present ministry position before you. What legacy did they leave behind? What opportunities or obstacles does their legacy present to you?

Questions for Lead Pastors or Ministry Directors

1. In this chapter I cited four core elements of credibility (integrity, intent, capabilities, and results). Think of the young leaders who work with you and ask, "In which of the core elements are they the strongest?"

2. What do you do to make your young leaders feel part of your leadership team?

Recommendations for Lead Pastors or Ministry Directors

1. As a staff, read and discuss the first chapters of the book *The Speed of Trust*, by Covey.

2. When you are with young leaders one-to-one, affirm them verbally by letting them know of their strengths in this area of credibility.

3. Let the young minister preach as often as possible.

4. Ask for the young minister's input into the formation of the church vision.

5. Put the young minister in various roles—help others see him in a different role.

6. Urge staff members to encourage the young ministers, as Paul encouraged Timothy.

Challenge #4

Dealing with Expectations

Have you ever said to yourself, "I never expected this," or "That certainly was a surprise?" Often, life has a way of not fitting in to our expectations.

What are some of the common expectations that turn out differently than we expect?

Expectations Regarding the Flexibility Needed in Ministry

I've joked with many over the years that perhaps we should add a tenth fruit of the Spirit, as listed in Galatians 5:22, 23, and that it should be the fruit of "flexibility." The need for flexibility in ministry is under-rated.

The need for flexibility shows up in a number of areas. As missionaries, Sherie and I had to move fourteen times in our first eleven years of ministry, due to visa issues, civil disruptions, and medical emergencies. One time we had only two hours notice before we had to leave our apartment.

For some ministers, the needed flexibility has to do with the daily schedule. One minister said this about the need for flexibility in ministry:

> Too many [ministers] are too rigid. One minister's wife insisted that their kids had to be in bed by seven each night. As a result of that expectation, she was not able to get

involved in ministry at all at night. That created a problem because in churches, ministries often meet at night.

For some ministers, the needed flexibility has to do with the people they work with or answer to. One young minister recalled a time when she was arbitrarily "let go" in her church ministry. One day she had a job, and the next day she didn't, through no apparent fault of her own and with little explanation:

> I was leading a youth ministry in [name of church], and someone in authority came to me and said, "We don't need you anymore." And I no longer had that job. Long story short ... I didn't do anything wrong, but I had to leave that ministry because they felt they didn't need me anymore. That event was almost enough to make me quit the ministry altogether. Those were my kids, my youth group, that I was ministering to. It is sad when someone can come in and arbitrarily dictate God's will like that.... I concluded that it was time to quit.

Fortunately, she was able to secure a full-time ministry in another nearby church and remains there today. But for her, dealing with the uncertainty of ministry in that particular situation was difficult to take, as I think it would be for me, too.

I hope that you don't have to move fourteen times in eleven years and that you don't ever hear, "we don't need you anymore." But learning to be flexible in ministry will certainly help you.

Ministry is Less Satisfying than Expected

For some young ministers, ministry is not as satisfying as they expected it to be. I asked the following question of many I interviewed: "Have you had any surprises in full-time ministry?" One minister had this to say,

> Ministry is not as busy as I expected it to be. I grew up in a pastor's family. Every day was busy. We had

Bible studies, various kinds of meetings, it was hands on, etc.—the day was full. But here [he was the music minister at his church] we have only one service per week. I feel cooped up in my office.

Ministry is Less Productive than Expected

I asked an experienced minister what challenges he is facing, and he simply said,

I've had to make adjustments in my expectations of ministry. Early in my ministry I expected that when I would preach, people would run to the altars to receive Christ. But that hasn't happened in my ministry.

Ministry is Much Tougher than Expected

I think that many who go into full-time ministry find that life as a minister is more demanding than they expected. One associate pastor said this:

Here in our church I know several who want to be youth pastors. But they are in love with an idealized form of ministry. We have tried to tell them what ministry is really like. There are challenges, costs to their family, and loneliness.

One of the reasons that some young ministers find it more challenging is that, as they grew up in church, they saw only the public aspect of their pastors. They saw their lead pastor or their youth pastor only when he was leading a service or preaching in front of a crowd and, as a result, they formed a skewed idea of what ministry is all about. It is remarkable to hear what some congregation members think of the pastor's job. Most lead pastors have had someone come up to them and say something ridiculous like this: "It must be nice to have a job where you preach on Sunday and Wednesday and then do nothing the rest of the week." Obviously (or maybe it's not so obvious), ministry is a lot more than the ninety minutes on Sunday morning or Wednesday evening. But, when young people see their minister only in a public setting, they can get a distorted perception of full-time ministry, and that can lead to disappointment when they enter the ministry.

Ministry is More Satisfying than Expected

Surely there are some who have been disappointed by the challenges they face in ministry. However, I feel compelled to ask, "Are there young ministers who have been pleasantly surprised in ministry?" Yes. For example, a minister in her late twenties who is enjoying her ministry position said, "I'm surprised that I'm in ministry today. I grew up in a pastor's family and I saw the effect on my family of being in the ministry." In contrast to those I cited earlier, she found that ministry was much more satisfying than she had expected.

Hoge and Wenger conducted a study of four professions to determine, among other things, the level of satisfaction that each had in their work. The four professions were minister, lawyer, physician, and social worker.

Hoge and Wenger cite four factors that influence the levels of satisfaction for members of those professions:

1. Meaning - Making a difference in other people's lives; devotion to a valuable cause.
2. Recognition - Being respected, esteemed by others
3. Autonomy - Freedom to determine daily schedule and priorities
4. Remuneration - Salary

Ministers reported a high level of meaning and autonomy, a medium level of recognition, and a low level of salary (in comparison with the other professions).

Hoge and Wenger found that the members of three of the four professions said they had a high level of satisfaction in their work; the exception was lawyers. Hoge and Wenger state that the lawyers "...have experienced a gradual diminution in career satisfaction over the last 20 years."[13]

Hoge and Wenger found that lawyers are paid better than ministers and social workers but do not find as much satisfaction as those two groups. On the other hand, ministers are paid less than the other three professions but consistently find satisfaction in their work. In my personal discussions with ministers, I find that the overwhelming percentage find a great sense of meaning in their work.

Expectations Regarding Your Readiness to Minister

When asked about the greatest challenges for those who are just starting out in ministry, a veteran missionary couple replied that young ministers should deal with their personality dysfunctions before jumping into ministry.

> Everybody has dysfunctions, insecurities, or things in their personalities they need to work on. It is best to let God work on those a lot before jumping into ministry because, once you're in ministry, those things rise to the surface and show up in your behavior. You'll never be perfect and have no issues to deal with, but you should let God take care of as many issues as possible before full-time ministry.

Once you are involved in your ministry, all kinds of "stuff" can be exposed in your life that can really hurt your ministry. As I reflect on my early years in ministry, and as I reflect on the young ministers with whom I've worked, some of the common dysfunctional behaviors that I have observed are:

- Insecurities
- Lack of respect for protocol
- Lack of respect for authority
- Placing too much confidence in those in leadership over us
- Expecting everyone to accept our vision; seeing little need to sell our vision
- Selfishness in marriage relationship and other relationships
- Too quick to speak and too quick to anger
- Overly ambitious (centered in ourselves, not God)

It is easy to say, "Let God deal with your dysfunctions," but it is more difficult to actually come to terms with them and let God deal with them. Often, I don't even recognize my dysfunctions. It usually takes a jolt of some kind for me to see them. That jolt may be a confrontation, a loss of a friend or relationship, getting fired, or the conviction of the Holy Spirit.

Our response to this challenge should not be to hold back from ministry, but rather to do all we can to be prepared for it, not only in terms of education and formal preparation, but also in terms of our personalities and relationships. The latter kind of preparation is the more difficult kind, for it goes right to the core of our self-perception and to breaking habits we have practiced for years. But doing that kind of work also prepares us wonderfully for ministry.

Expectations Regarding the Routine in Ministry

I find that young ministers are out to change the world, and I'm thankful for the energy and vision they bring to the ministry. In our world we need that. But you may be surprised at how much of ministry is just handling the mundane details of ministry. One twenty-nine-year-old youth pastor said, "Some come into youth work not expecting to have to do administrative work. But they are surprised. It takes a lot of administrative work to do youth events."

I recall speaking to a young lead pastor at a church. He was frustrated. He went into the ministry to minister to people, but he was spending most of his time doing something else: "I feel like I'm pastoring this church building, not the people. I spend most of my time dealing with the details of this building."

Another aspect of the mundane in the ministry occurs in a local church. It is the routine aspect of ministry. Every local church has a weekly schedule. Here's a common schedule in churches: Sunday - church services, Monday - day off, Tuesday - staff meeting, Wednesday - midweek services, Thursday - hospital visitation, Friday - intense preparation for Sunday, Saturday - church activities. Then, you repeat the process. You could say that in the local church you do the same thing fifty-two times each year. Fortunately, there is variety, including vacations, conferences, campaigns, and guest speakers, but there is a routine in ministry. The person who enters the ministry looking for continual excitement will not last. Those who endure in the ministry perceive the meaningful events that happen during the routine.

Expectations Regarding Politics in the Ministry

Politics play a part in ministry. I am not referring to whether you are a Democrat, Independent, or Republican. I'm referring to the political processes at work in your local church or in your ministry.

It is easy, as a young minister, to lose your zeal when you see what you perceive to be decisions in your setting that are made on the basis of "politics" and not on more worthy criteria.

Before continuing in this discussion, it would be helpful to define what I mean by politics. Years ago I taught a course titled, "Power and Politics in the Ministry," and I think the definition I used in that course is useful:

> Politics: "The informal and sometimes emotion-driven process of allocating limited resources and working out goals, decisions, and actions in an environment of people with different and competing interests and personalities."[14]

I like this definition because it does not vilify the process of politics. Politics, as defined here, occurs wherever people live and work together. Politics occurs, according to Dobson and Dobson, when there are "differing and competing interests and personalities." Thus, politics occurs in a variety of life-settings. It occurs in a family of father, mother, and children. It occurs in a Sunday school class, in board meetings, and in the church pastoral staff relationships. Really, anywhere you have personal relationships, you also have a certain level of politics. It's not an evil process. It's just a fact of life.

How does politics show up in the ministry? I have three quotes from youth pastors below that reveal the ways politics operate in churches.

Quote #1: "Youth pastors want more of the church budget."

I included this quote to call attention to what the "politics" definition referred to as the process of "allocating limited resources..." The entire budget process in a local church is a political process. Once again, it is not negative in and of itself. Somebody has to make the final decision of how much of the financial pie goes to each ministry in the local church.

Quote #2: "I grew up in the church, so I know how things work in a church setting."

A pastor's kid stated this and the inflection of his voice said just as much as the words he used. As he was growing up he observed the processes at work in the local church and he concluded that there were concealed maneuvers working below the visible level.

Our "politics" definition spoke of people "with different and competing interests and personalities." That describes people in our churches. I am not saying that church people are bad. Not at all. Most are good people, but each defaults to looking at church decisions from his or her own perspective, and that creates a political process.

Quote #3: "I've seen a couple of my friends step out of ministry. One stepped out because, when conflict arose, he felt that his pastor did not support him. Sometimes we feel like everyone is against us."

It is tough when your lead pastor does not seem to support you. A common situation in churches is when people take sides regarding the effectiveness of a certain pastoral staff member and the lead pastor gets caught in the middle. Then, the working out of "goals, decisions, and actions in an environment of people with different and competing interests and personalities" occurs.

Those are just three facets of church and ministry politics.

The problem occurs when we expect that just because we are in the church, this "political" process does not occur. After all, the Scriptures indicate that we are appointed to exalted roles and given distinguished titles. We are appointed as Christ's "ambassadors." We are called "saints." Here's how Peter described the local church: "But ye are a chosen generation, a royal priesthood, an holy nation, a peculiar people; that ye should shew forth the praises of him who hath called you out of darkness into his marvelous light" (1 Peter 2:9, KJV). Those descriptions don't harmonize with "politics" because we have seen so many bad examples of "politics" in our world.

Former U. S. President Richard Nixon, who was well-known for the Watergate scandal, calls attention to the negative aspect of politics when he says in his book *Leaders*, "We honor leaders for what they achieve, but we often prefer to close our eyes to the way they achieve it."[15] It is ironic that Nixon would write this given his central role in the Watergate scandal. But he makes a good point. As Christians, we may "close our eyes" to impure processes because those processes often do not fit with our calling to be godly and holy, or at least it is not a process we can be proud of.

We must see the difference between the negative aspects of politics and the neutral aspects. The negative aspects include manipulation, impure motives, and even bribes. Those, of course, should not be in the church. They should be rejected as improper for God's people. The neutral aspect, however, involves an understanding that good people have differing perspectives on church decisions, and that somebody must make the final decision.

Political situations, as defined above, are realities. But your reaction to them will make or break you. You need to be careful that you don't get sucked into the negative attitudes that sometimes arise in reaction to the decisions that are made in your ministry situation. Paul's advice to Timothy applies here: "Keep a close watch on yourself and on your teaching. Stay true to what is right, and God will save you and those who hear you" (1 Tim. 4:16, NLT).

Watch your attitude when it comes to decisions made in your ministry context. Don't get caught up in a negative "political" atmosphere. Keep a godly perspective.

Dealing with Others' Expectations of You

Like people in many other occupations, those in full-time ministry sometimes struggle with the variety of expectations that others have of them. Listen to what one youth pastor said: "Everybody has expectations for me as a youth pastor. Students want entertainment, parents want me to do miracles [with their young people], and lead pastors want numbers." And, in response to all these expectations, youth pastors sometimes say, "This is not much fun." Others youth pastors say, "Yea, I understand your expectations for my ministry, but what about my opinion and my expectations for this ministry? Aren't they important, too?"

Expectations Regarding Team Leadership in Churches

Some young ministers feel they've been set up. They read in the latest ministry books that today's trend is toward team leadership in churches. They read that organizations, including churches, are moving from hierarchical models to flat models of leadership. They read that older leaders are more transparent and more willing to listen to young leaders than they've been in the past. And then they get their first ministry position and find that reality does not match what is being written in the books. (Apparently, their lead pastor has not read those books.)

More often than not, I think what has happened is that the lead pastor or director is aware of the trends and would like to move toward more of a team leadership model, but that goal gets lost in the day-to-day details of ministry. Life and ministry move along at a fast clip. It's not that the top leader is against team leadership, it's just that it's easier to talk about than to implement.

But, from your perspective, what you expected was not fulfilled. You want more opportunity for input than is allowed. You want more time with your director or lead pastor. But life's busy pace causes those dreams to be left behind.

What are some of the solutions to dealing with these expectations?

Understand Expectations in Advance

An obvious solution is to know the expectations that others have toward you. For example, when interviewing for a ministry position, identify the expectations you bring to the job and the expectations of your boss and your spouse and family. Too often we assume that we know what is expected of us, and then we get blindsided. When you interview, don't assume, ask. Make the expectations explicit. This does not mean you won't get surprised once you start your job, but you can minimize the number of unstated expectations by asking about them.

Remember that Each Ministry Culture Has Its Specific Expectations

Expectations differ from church culture to church culture, or from one work environment to another. When we switch ministries, we often expect others to have the same or similar expectations that we encountered in our last place. But we must remember that each ministry culture has its specific expectations.

Identify the expectations in your current setting. How good is the fit with your current ministry? Are you a round peg in a square hole? Where is there alignment? Where is there a lack of synchronization?

Understand How Expectations Change over Time

The expectations that others have toward you will change over time. Think of it, do you expect the same thing of a twenty-five-year old man as you do of a sixty-five-year old man? Of course, that is an extreme example. But it illustrates that our expectations change over the years.

It is helpful to ask yourselves a couple of questions.

- What requirements were stated when you interviewed for your present position?
- Have those expectations changed over the years?

For example, perhaps when you interviewed for your job, your kids were infants and toddlers. But now your kids are older and less dependent upon you, and, therefore, perhaps the lead pastor expects you to attend more church functions. Or, perhaps your church has helped fund your continuing education over the years. Have others' expectations toward you changed as a result of the funding assistance or the increased education? Unearth the expectations; discover them. What you don't know can hurt you.

Identify Unrealistic Expectations You Impose on Yourself

Unrealistic expectations can come from a variety of sources. Sometimes, the unrealistic expectations are our own.

When my wife and I were studying French in Quebec, one evening we turned on the TV and watched a show in French similar to The Dave Letterman Show. One of the guests was a man from a French Overseas Territory in the Caribbean. This man was invited to the show because he claimed he could break open a coconut using his teeth. I doubt you've ever tried that before, but it would be quite a feat. When we lived in the South Pacific, we used machetes to open coconuts and even that is not easy. The host invited his guest onto the stage, had him sit down, and asked a few questions about his work and family. Then the host announced, "Now, ladies and gentlemen, our guest will open a coconut using only his teeth."

The guest took center stage. A stage hand gave him a coconut and he began biting it like a dog bites a bone. I don't know if the guest was overconfident of his abilities, or perhaps the coconut that day was harder than your normal, run-of-the-mill coconut, but try as he might, the guest could not crack that coconut. He bit and bit but that coconut would not crack. After about a minute of biting, his gums began bleeding. But he was not about to give up; he continued biting. Then his eyes began watering—from the pain, I assume. And then he cut his lip and it began to bleed. I felt sorry for the guy who at this point was bleeding with eyes watering as he continued to bite the coconut, but it never cracked. It was really a bizarre scene. Finally, to my relief, the host broke in and stopped the ordeal, like a referee calling an end to a boxing match before the losing boxer gets killed. The host was kind in thanking the guest for his attempt, and after the audience graciously clapped for him, the program transitioned to a commercial. My thought was that the guy was crazy to try such a feat. On the other hand, Sherie and I were glued to the tube as we watched the entire ten-minute segment. Here it is, twenty-five years later, and I still remember it, so I assume the producers figured it was "good TV" because it was so entertaining.

I think you know what I'm leading to. Sometimes our expectations toward ourselves are unrealistic, like the coconut man. Okay, maybe we aren't quite that extreme, but we can fall into the trap of expecting way too much of ourselves. I remember hearing myself preach for the first time and being dismayed at how bad it was compared to the preaching of my pastors as I grew up. Of course, what I had forgotten was that I was twenty years old and my pastors had been preaching longer than I'd been alive. Sometimes we need to let up a little and cut ourselves some slack.

The result of giving in to unrealistic expectations is that we lose the God-designed balance that will enable us to endure in ministry. Identify the urges and beliefs within you that drive you to imbalances in your life. Are you trying to please God, or are you trying to overcome some unmet need in your life? Taking time to reflect on these things can be enlightening.

Jesus said that his yoke was easy and his burden was light. We should not take that to mean that we shouldn't work hard. We should work hard, but we should also maintain balance in our lives between work, family, and our personal lives. Sometimes the burden we have taken on has nothing to do with what God expects of us. God gets unjustly blamed for a lot of things.

I think the following verse has application to dealing with our expectations: "Therefore, strengthen your feeble arms and weak knees. Make level paths for your feet so that the lame may not be disabled, but rather healed" (Hebrews 12:12, NIV). Making "level paths" for our feet includes assuring that our expectations are realistic and God-pleasing. When we have healthy expectations, others who are following us will be more likely to have healthy expectations toward themselves, too, and will endure in their spiritual lives and in their ministries.

Questions for Young Leaders

1. How is full-time ministry different from what you expected?

2. In what ways are you okay with the way full-time ministry has turned out for you? What do you like most about full-time ministry?

3. In what ways are you struggling with unfulfilled expectations in ministry?

4. If you are married, in what ways is full-time ministry different from what your spouse expected? Have you discussed those expectations with your spouse?

5. How satisfied are you with each of the following aspects of ministry? (Circle one)

A. Meaning: making a difference in other people's lives; devotion to a valuable cause

Not satisfied   Somewhat satisfied   Very satisfied

B. Recognition: being respected, esteemed by others

Not satisfied   Somewhat satisfied   Very satisfied

C. Autonomy: freedom to determine daily schedule and priorities

Not satisfied   Somewhat satisfied   Very satisfied

D. Remuneration: salary

Not satisfied   Somewhat satisfied   Very satisfied

Questions for Lead Pastors or Ministry Directors

1. What expectations do you have of the young ministers who work with you?

2. Are any of these expectations not being met? If so, what are they, and is the young minister's obstacle a lack of knowledge/skills/understanding, or is it a lack of will?

3. Is there anything you could do to help your young leader fulfill those expectations?

4. Most likely you have had times when full-time ministry exceeded your expectations, and times when full-time ministry left you with unfulfilled expectations. Reflect on and list both sets of expectations.

5. What has enabled you to persevere in ministry?

Recommendations for Lead Pastors or Ministry Directors

1. In a staff meeting, or in a one-to-one meeting with a young minister, broach this subject of expectations. Be willing to share how ministry has exceeded your expectations, and how it has left you with unfulfilled expectations. Describe your own journey.

2. Initiate a discussion on "politics in the church" and how you deal with such politics. Give permission to the young leader to openly express his viewpoint of the politics he sees.

Challenge # 5

Working Successfully with the Opportunities Available

Think of the variables you would use to describe your ideal work situation. Maybe it has to do with salary, a particular geographic location, or specific qualities you would want in your boss. Perhaps in your ideal work situation you would have a lot of autonomy or the freedom to be wildly creative.

Now, take a moment to reflect on your current and actual work situation. How does it measure up to your ideal work situation? If you're like most people, there is a gap between your ideal and your actual work situation. How are you responding to that gap?

Whatever your circumstances, keep this in mind: Your attitude toward them is more important than your actual circumstances. Finding fulfillment in our work has less to do with having an ideal work situation and more to do with choosing to make the best of our circumstances.

There are tough situations in ministry. One older minister talked about a difficult situation:

> Early in my ministry I almost quit. I was frustrated. I was an associate pastor here at [name of church] working for [name of pastor]. He was a tough boss, he was insensitive, and he was very disorganized. Then a pastor friend called and raked me over the coals. He knew my feelings. He was like a father. He said, "Do you feel like you are the only one frustrated with ministry? Listen.

> When God is finished with you there at the church it
> will be like he gives you a bill of divorcement. You will
> know when it is time to go."

Our natural reaction to tough situations is to flee to another ministry position, just as this minister wanted to do. That is the easy road (at least until you get into the same situation again). The challenge when faced with a tough work situation is to work as successfully as you can with the opportunities you do have, to make the best of a less-than-perfect situation. You must be willing to ask some hard questions: God, do you have me in this situation for a purpose? Do you want me to remain in this situation so you can use it to develop me into the person you want me to be?

God began teaching me this lesson when I was about sixteen. I was reading a book by an author with a unique nickname. His name was Charlie "Tremendous" Jones. I don't recall the book's title now, but I do recall one cartoon in the book. The cartoon was of a man sitting at a desk with a two-foot-high pile of papers in front of him calling for his attention. Instead of a look of dread—that's the way I would feel with such a pile of work to do—he had a smile and was enthusiastically shouting something—was it "wonderful" or "terrific?" The message of the cartoon was that though you've got a ton of unpleasant work to do, you can still approach life at that moment with joy. At the same time I was reading that book I was reading another one, *Prison to Praise*, a popular book in those days. The author's main idea was that when we face difficult circumstances and constantly complain about them we will find that our spirits are in a spiritual prison. But if we can learn to praise God in the midst of those circumstances, our spirits will be freed and that freedom will actually help us persevere even when the circumstances don't improve. At that time in my life I was facing some difficult situations and I took the authors' lessons to heart and learned to praise God in difficult situations, and then to remain in that situation and see God work through it. Those were foundational lessons that have sustained me through many years.

I've met leaders who were facing tough, seeming impossible, situations but who were applying the "prison to praise" perspective. Some were hoping to turn around a youth group that was in shambles. Others were pastoring a church or directing a ministry whose future seemed hopeless. But they were making the best of it. And, instead of dreading their ministries, they had a deep joy as they worked through the situations.

While in prison, Joseph continued to serve God with a good attitude and eventually God brought him through. Paul and Silas sang while in prison chains and God released them. They serve as great examples.

Working with a Difficult Boss

More than one minister has taken a job as youth pastor or assistant pastor, and then discovered that the lead pastor is not the person he or she expected him to be. The complaints I hear most often are that the lead pastor is insecure, disorganized, has no vision for the church, or that there is some kind of personality conflict between the assistant and the lead pastor. (Of course, it works the other way, too—there are leaders who discover that their new assistant is not what they expected.)

One man said that he once worked with a lead pastor who, in the middle of their conversation in the lead pastor's office, would pick up his phone and call someone on a topic totally unrelated to their situation. The lead pastor expected the associate to wait for him there in the office until he finished his phone conversation. And this occurred thirty-five years ago, long before the days when cell phones could interrupt us 24/7.

What do you do when you find yourself working for a difficult boss but you conclude that quitting is not an option? Your work with the situation as it is.

McCall, Lombardo, and Morrison, in their book, *The Lessons of Experience*, relate the story of Gene, a business executive who had a difficult boss. Then they make the following observation:

> Gene's experience and the lessons he learned from it reflects the experience of many executives who, at some point, found themselves at the mercy of a boss with few redeeming qualities. Unable to immediately extricate themselves from the situation, they were left with little choice but to find a way to make the relationship work: understanding your adversary, coping with what he threw at you, and learning what *not* to do.[16]

If a minister can learn to make the best of a seemingly impossible situation that has no practical way out, such as working with a difficult boss, then he has learned a valuable lesson. After all, we never know what life will throw at us.

Learning the Lessons

One of the challenges that young leaders face is actually learning lessons in the midst of unpleasant circumstances. Sometimes we know there is a lesson to be learned but we can't quite articulate it. This challenge is one we face throughout life, but it is particularly important for young leaders.

When we face a tough situation and we know we should learn something from it, asking ourselves penetrating questions can often help us learn the lessons that will help us later on. The questions make up what I call an "Experience Audit." This audit occurs when you take time to reflect on the lessons you are learning or have recently learned in some specific experience. Some of the helpful questions in an Experience Audit include:

Auditing Yourself:
As a result of this experience...
+ What have you discovered about yourself?
+ What kind of people respond to, and do not respond to, your leadership?
+ What causes you to lose patience?
+ What have you learned that you do well, and do not do well?
+ What have you decided you should and should not do in the future?

Auditing Your Job Situation:
As a result of this experience...
+ What are the elements of this job situation that you liked and that you want for future jobs?
+ What are the elements of this job situation that you didn't like and you don't want for future jobs?
+ What steps can you take to set yourself up for success in the future?

Auditing Your Boss Preference:
As a result of this experience...

+ What kind of boss do you work well with? What kind of boss do you not work well with?

+ What kind of boss do you want to be? What lessons have you learned about being a boss that you want to incorporate into your behavior as a boss?

+ Have you learned that you would prefer to be your own boss (and start your own ministry), and that you have the capacities to pull that off? If so, what factors figure into those conclusions?

Auditing Your Level of Surrender:
As a result of this experience...

+ What areas of your life did God ask you to surrender to Him that had not been surrendered before?

+ Were there areas of your life where God called you to take greater steps of faith? If so, what were those areas? What was your response? Where did you resist?

God is working within us, to develop us. He uses the circumstances of our lives to move us toward maturity. We are focused on being productive, on numbers, and other metrics. God is concerned with those things (consider, for example, the parable of the one lost sheep), but He is also concerned with developing us to be more like Him.

The opportunities presented to us are tests. Sometimes the most important question is this: "Will I stay put, work hard, and persevere so that I can see how God will work in my situation to achieve His will for me?"

Robert Clinton refers to one kind of situation that is difficult for leaders to face. He calls it *leadership backlash*. He defines *leadership backlash* as "the negative reactions of others to a course of action taken by a leader once ramifications develop from his decision."[17]

Moses is an example of a leader who faced a *leadership backlash*. He received a vision from God to lead the children of Israel from Egypt to the Promised Land. As they were moving in the direction of his vision, the Israelites experienced hard times and complained to Moses. Although they originally agreed to Moses' vision, they eventually blamed him for having taken them out of Egypt. This *leadership backlash* caused Moses to look to God for help and further direction.

Robert Clinton says "the primary lesson for the leader [in a leadership backlash] is learning submission to God. This lesson is often lost, though, because of the other problems of authority, relationships, and conflict.... God uses complications to develop inner-life maturity. Leadership backlash is a form of integrity testing in which the leader's actual motivation can be revealed."[18]

Paul writes to Timothy in 1 Timothy 6:6 (KJV), "*But godliness with contentment is great gain.*" Though the context there deals with money, I think we can apply that lesson of contentment to the tough circumstances of our lives. If we can be godly and be content in a difficult situation—a situation where God has told us to stay put—that is great gain.

There is a Time to Leave

Though I believe that all of us need to grow in our ability to persevere, there certainly is a time to leave a ministry position. Many ministers who are facing less-than-ideal circumstances leave their ministries. Many do so for good reasons.

The following are some of the reasons leaders, particularly young leaders, leave a ministry:

+ They do not fit the patterns expected of someone in their position.
+ Their vision does not match the vision of the leader.
+ They have rough edges that cover up their good leadership qualities and potential.
+ They believe they are over-used and under–developed.
+ They are placed in non-challenging roles.
+ They are denied input into the organization's decision making.[19]

This chapter is all about making the best of your present situation. Yet I acknowledge that there is a time to leave a ministry and move on. How does a young minister know when it is time to move on?

As you think through your options, you will find value in asking yourself penetrating questions that will help you process the information you have:

Do I expect too much from myself or others?

I find it is common for young ministers to expect their followers to grasp their ministry vision quickly, and when this doesn't happen the ministers become discouraged or are ready to move on. Getting people to buy in to your vision requires persistence. Consider this fact: God built His vision into your heart over the course of months and years, but we unrealistically expect our followers to "catch it" in weeks or days, or even after one vision talk. Perhaps you should stay and revise your expectations.

Am I avoiding some difficult people, situations, or needs?

Most leaders don't enjoy plunging into situations with difficult people or situations, but they learn how to handle these situations. If you are thinking of leaving due to a difficult situation, what will you do the next time you face a similar situation? If, at a young age, you learn to overcome these kinds of challenges with God's help, that insight will help you in the future.

Am I living in fear of change?

Anytime we act due to fear we risk making a mistake. Hebrews 10:35 says, *"Do not throw away this confident trust in the Lord, no matter what happens."*

Have I lost respect and trust in leadership?

If you have lost respect and trust in those who lead you, then it may be time to move on. Then again, if you expect all leaders to be perfect or nearly perfect, you will be disappointed again. Perhaps you need to revise your expectations of those who lead in your ministry. How do we know the difference? I would say that if you see a pattern developing over time, it may be time to leave. For example, if you have been disappointed repeatedly, it may be time to move on.

Have I become lost in the busyness of routine and of keeping my head above water?

This is normally not a reason to leave. Periodically, every leader needs to reevaluate his or her schedule and ask if it is sustainable over the long haul. Prune your schedule and priorities regularly.

You may decide that you shouldn't leave, but instead stay and try to overhaul your current ministry position. Following are suggestions that may help you to overhaul your role and your identity:

- ◆ Renew relationships.
- ◆ Construct a different office setup or create a fresh environment.
- ◆ Ask to get away for a few days.
- ◆ Add new resources to your ministry.
- ◆ Discover an interest not related to your ministry role.[20]

Those Who Made a Transition

Ultimately, after thinking through all of your options, you may decide that it is time to leave your present ministry. Over the years, I've observed friends who have left their present ministry to do something else. I would sort them into three groups:

The first group consists of those who left their ministry and simply went on to become an effective leader in another existing ministry. For example, a youth pastor resigns and then takes a youth pastor position at another church. Most of those who prayed seriously and took their time before making the move found that once they were established in their new ministry, they were glad they had moved on. The exceptions are those who had a kneejerk reaction to a negative situation, acted in haste, and resigned.

A second group consists of those who left their position in a church or ministry and went on to found their own ministry. I've coached a number of ministers through this transition and the one variable that makes a big difference between success and failure is whether the minister is able and willing to raise the funds and financial commitments to not only start the new ministry but sustain it. I've discovered most ministers who create their ministry are clear on their vision, but it is the funding that is the greatest challenge. Too many seem to move ahead prematurely.

A third group consists of those who left their ministry position, and then actually left vocational ministry. They are now businessmen or in some other occupation. I would further divide this group into two groups.

First, there are those who left the ministry in their early years of ministry because they tried it and found that they didn't like it. They didn't leave the ministry because they wanted to get rich, nor did they leave because they were mistreated by their boss. They simply decided, after a year or two in ministry, that God was calling them to do something else. They are thankful for their time in full-time ministry, but they discovered it was not for them. I've found that most of the guys and gals I've known who've done this become great assets in their local church. They leave ministry to go into another occupation, but they continue to be faithful in service to their local church. I conclude that they made the correct decision.

Second, there are those who leave vocational ministry because in their early ministry years their boss, the church board, or their church people mistreated them. Certainly, there are many unhealthy churches and leaders out there. I went to college with a guy who became a youth pastor about the same time I did. While my experience was positive, his was extremely negative. In fact, he had negative experiences in the first two churches where he worked as a youth pastor. I lost track of him and I thought for sure he would leave the ministry, but recently I learned that he is still in ministry and doing well. His experience does not nullify the fact that many young ministers leave the ministry due to mistreatment. Part of the reason for this book is to prepare young ministers for those kinds of experiences.

What can we do to help our colleagues facing a tough ministry situation? Perhaps you are working with a fellow assistant pastor who is debating whether to leave or stay in his present position. Or, perhaps you are just a friend of a fellow leader who is struggling with whether to leave or stay.

Robert Clinton provides a word of direction for us: "Frequently at the heart of the problems lies the need for people of influence in the organization to see this problem and take steps to retain these potential leaders."[21]

Clinton goes on to describe what he calls "The Sponsor Gap."

> The sponsor gap refers to the need for high level leaders
> to intervene in a mentoring sense with potential leaders
> well below their level to encourage, protect, enable, link to
> resources and otherwise relate to the potential leader so as
> to keep them in the organization and to develop them.[22]

Early in his ministry the man we know now as the Apostle Paul was struggling to gain credibility among the believers in Jerusalem. It was Barnabas who used his influence to sponsor Paul. Only then did the apostles accept Paul. (Acts 9:26-28)

If you know a leader who is struggling to find his niche in a church or ministry, ask yourself the following questions:

+ Have you taken the time to pray with that leader?
  Sometimes a leader just needs to know that someone is walking with them through the struggle.

+ What can you do to encourage, protect, enable, or resource the leader?
  What influence or other resource do you have to help that leader?

Young leaders, remember that older sponsors are not the only ones who can assist those facing tough situations. I would encourage those who are age twenty to thirty to come alongside colleagues who are facing challenging circumstances and help them focus on finding God in their situation. Young ministers can come alongside other young ministers and provide a different perspective that may prove to be pivotal for them.

The Flesh Act

I remember the days when it was easy to make a transition from one job to the next one. I was young, single, and I could fit all my possessions into my Camaro. All that was necessary to move on was to give the proper notice to my boss and then when moving day came, move all my belongings from my apartment to my car in a few hours and drive away. Now, life has become much more complicated.

Younger ministers often find it easier than older ministers to move through a transition to the next step in their lives and ministries. The younger minister may be single, or married with no kids, enabling him to pick up and move quicker than older ministers who have a family with kids in school. However, this increased mobility can be hazardous. We can act impatiently, without adequate deliberation and prayer. Clinton cautions leaders to be wary of what he calls "the flesh act."

The flesh act refers to those instances in a leader's life when guidance is presumed and decisions are made either hastily or without proper discernment of God's choice.

Clinton warns that such decisions can result in "ramifications that later affect ministry and life negatively."[23]

An example of the flesh act occurred in the life of King Saul. He was instructed to wait until Samuel arrived before presenting a sacrifice to the Lord. But he felt he couldn't wait, so he committed a flesh act by offering the sacrifice himself. Because of his flesh act, King Saul eventually lost his kingdom. The Lord was not pleased, to say the least.

God rebuked Saul through Samuel:

> *"You fool! You have disobeyed the commandment of the Lord your God. He was planning to make you and your descendents kings of Israel forever, but now your dynasty must end, for the Lord wants a man who will obey him.* (1 Samuel 13:13, 14, The Living Bible)

As a result of this flesh act, Saul indeed experienced ramifications that later affected his ministry and life negatively.

What, when, and *how* are all important facets of guidance. Sometimes we know what God wants us to do but we fail to consider the timing. Perhaps He wants us to wait patiently for His time. Also, we may know what God has called us to and even the timing, but we should pray about "how" God wants us to do it. Clinton cites several ways that the flesh act is done:

> Presumptuous faith assumes God will do something that He has not communicated and can lead to a flesh act. In major decisions, acting without consulting God often results in a flesh act. Failing to act or choosing a human alternative, instead of doing something God has pointed out, are also flesh acts.[24]

In my early days of ministry I often heard a song that connected with me numerous times as it played on the Christian radio stations. The words reminded me to be patient and wait on God's timing, something I needed to hear often in those days.

I must wait, wait, wait on the Lord.
I must wait, wait, wait on the Lord.
Learn my lessons well and in His timing He will tell me
what to do, where to go, what to say.

One time, while I was waiting on God's timing in a ministry situation, I found myself sitting in rush-hour freeway traffic in Los Angeles. Somebody aptly coined the word, "Carmageddon," to describe the traffic situation here in L.A. As I looked around at all the cars, it was like the traffic was mirroring my life. The traffic was moving slowly, just like my life seemed to be moving so slowly. And then over the radio came this song reminding me to wait on Him. God used that song on that day to remind me that His timing is good and I could trust Him.

Remaining Faithful

One older minister encouraged young ministers to be faithful, and to realize that as they are faithful, opportunities will come to them. He referred to Jesus' story of the servant, and then talked about the differences in generations.

The Story of the Servant:

> When a servant comes in from plowing or taking care of sheep, he doesn't just sit down and eat. He must first prepare his master's meal and serve him his supper before eating his own. And the servant is not even thanked, because he is merely doing what he is supposed to do. In the same way, when you obey me you should say, "We are not worthy of praise. We are servants who have simply done our duty." (Luke 17:7-10, NLT)

The leader had this to say about young ministers:

> The servant shouldn't expect the master to thank him. Former generations got their strokes from what they produced. For some it was how many widgets they mass produced. Today, the younger generation ... they want representation. But here is the deal—if you do your work

and are faithful, then God will put you at the table. Work hard, stay faithful, and don't expect to be thanked for doing what you should be doing. Do your work and do it well, and you will be at the table.

As I reflected on that quote, I thought about a verse that reflects a quality of God that I relied on early in my ministry, and continue to rely on today.

"For no one on earth—from east or west, or even from the wilderness—can raise another person up. It is God alone who judges; he decides who will rise and who will fall" (Psalm 75:6-7, NLT).

The quality of God as a just judge is one that we can rely on as ministers of the gospel. If we concentrate on pleasing God, He will cause others to notice us. He is the best publicist we could have.

Consider how one older minister learned this lesson:

I was fired from my first youth pastor job. My wife was seven months pregnant. Nobody would hire me. Then I heard that [name of a pastor] was looking for a youth pastor. I interviewed for the position. After the interview I thought I was a shoo-in. But [the pastor] told me, "You're not the youth pastor we are looking for." Remember this came after I'd been fired in my first youth pastorate. I was twenty-five. I thought I'd been blackballed by my denominational leaders. But I found a position, remained faithful, and worked hard."

Today, years later, that minister is the leader of a large and effective ministry.

Summing Up

I conclude this chapter with several axioms for success in ministry:

+ There are no perfect work situations.
+ God calls you to be faithful right where you are.
+ Learn the lessons God is trying to teach you.
+ God's timing is perfect.
+ Let God be sovereign.

Questions for Young Leaders

1. Describe your perfect work situation. Include job description, salary, geographic setting, colleagues, boss, and possibilities for the future.

2. How does your present situation fall short of that perfect work situation? How have you reacted to the shortcomings of your present situation? What biblical directives should you apply to your situation?

3. Find a godly confidant (preferably outside your work situation) and describe to him/her how you would like to improve your relationship with your boss. Then, ask your confidant for his/her opinion.

4. If you haven't answered this chapter's questions in the "Experience Audit," take time now to do so.

5. What real "bones do you have to pick" with your present work situation? Which of these may be eliminated if you talk with your boss?

6. How would looking at your situation from God's eternal perspective alter your own attitude?

Questions for Lead Pastors or Ministry Directors

1. Do you know a young minister who is in need of a sponsor? Can you sponsor him/her?
   A sponsor is a leader who intervenes in a mentoring sense with potential leaders well below their organizational level to encourage, protect, enable, link to resources, and otherwise relate to the potential leaders so as to keep them in the organization and to develop them.

2. What lessons did you learn in your less-than-perfect work situations?

3. What guidelines do you use to determine whether a minister should stay in or leave his present ministry position?

Recommendations for Lead Pastors or Ministry Directors

1. When young leaders share their challenges take time to pray with them.

2. Ask the young leaders who work with you, "How can I be a better boss?"

Challenge # 6

Learning How to Work with People

An early major challenge for young ministers is that of working well with people. As one minister said, "You can learn many skills such as how to balance a budget, how to change and replace church equipment, etc., but the challenging part of ministry is dealing with people."

In the local church, no two people are the same. As a minister, you have a front row on humanity. You get to see the variety of God's creation. And, as you know, that is both positive and negative.

It doesn't take long in ministry to realize that there are people you enjoy working with—you look forward to your interactions with them. But you are less enthusiastic about working with others. Perhaps you find them too demanding, or too intense, or they have some other quality that grates on you.

At the first church I pastored, one of the long-standing members and a former board member—I'll call him John (not his real name)— had quite a problem with anger. And his anger often displayed itself while he was driving his motorbike in our small town. One weekday, while we were having a prayer meeting at church, we heard John outside screaming at another driver, "Hey, when are you goin to learn to drive?" His outburst abruptly interrupted the spirit of our prayer time. That was the first time I heard or observed John's anger. We were patient with him and had many great times of fellowship with him, but I learned early on in ministry that working alongside him would be no piece of cake.

One of the challenges as we start out is learning to work with such a variety of people.

Ask yourself, what kind of people you've been accustomed to working with. If you've had experience working with a wide variety of people, you've had a broad and useful preparation for ministry. Most of us need to learn to be more flexible, particularly early on in ministry.

Paul's advice to Timothy revealed that Timothy would need to be flexible. In 2 Timothy 4:2b, Paul instructs Timothy to *"Patiently correct, rebuke, and encourage your people with good teaching."* Some would need correcting, some would need something stronger, such as a rebuke, and others would need encouraging. Our response should fit the need.

Application:
It might be good to stop and reflect for a moment. Who are the people in or around your ministry whose personalities grate on you? You will probably have no problem identifying them. Identify what it is that they do to irritate you, or whatever reaction they cause in you.

Philippians 4:8 tells us to think on the good things. So, after identifying the negative part of their personalities, try to identify several good things about them. Some recommend using the three-to-one ratio. For every negative trait you can think of, try to think of three good ones about them. Then, whenever you think of them, try to focus on the good things in their lives and ignore the bad things.

When Others Don't Get Your Vision

It is a great feeling when you receive a God-given vision for your ministry, communicate it to the people you are leading, have them catch the vision, and then move forward together. But often that vision process breaks down because the people just don't seem to catch your vision. Then, it is easy to blame them, as did the veteran pastor below:

> When I was first in ministry I would get frustrated and ask, "Why didn't the guy in the pew get it? Why was he not buying into my vision? What is wrong with him?"

That last question can be a trap. It may be true that the fault lies with the receiver of the vision, but I think that often it lies with the sender of the vision. The veteran pastor went on to explain:

But it is not his fault. I learned that I need to communicate more clearly and then continue to repeat myself more often, so that eventually the light goes on in the mind and spirit of the people I'm leading. Young guys find that others don't buy into their vision and they conclude, they (the people they are ministering to) don't get it and it is their fault. Instead young guys need to ask themselves, 'How can I communicate more effectively? How can I communicate so they embrace the vision?' "

As a young minister, I had to learn that my listeners' failure to comprehend my vision was not simply because I was working with those who were more traditional while I was more progressive. It had to do with me, whether I would communicate well, whether I had listened to them and incorporated their thoughts into the vision, and whether I would be patient.

An experienced minister reflected on the timing issue:

Another challenge facing young ministers is that though they have the ability to communicate, they may not understand God's timing. The older I get the more I understand His timing. We want it to happen now. For example, God has given me a passion for this ministry I am now leading. But I need to trust in God's timing, and not force it. When you force it, you alienate people. Surround yourself with people who believe you've heard from God, but who are willing to say, "Not yet." Ask, "Is it the right time?"

Normally, when it is God's timing for a ministry or project to move forward, we will see a convergence of the following four factors:

+ the heart (the emotional desires)
+ the circumstances (providential factors)
+ the church (confirmation from mature fellow Christians)
+ the Word of God

Sometimes we have three of the four and move forward. We have a God-given vision in our heart, the first factor. The circumstances line up with our vision, the second factor. And our vision is in accordance with the Word of God, the fourth factor. But normally it is wise to wait for others to confirm and get on board with your vision before moving forward. I say normally because through history there have been pioneers, such as Martin Luther, who had a God-given vision and surged forward despite great opposition from the church as a whole. But generally, it is best to move forward only when all factors converge. When we don't wait on the third factor—confirmation from mature fellow believers—we risk making a mistake.

Working with People Older Than You

As a young leader, much of your work is with those older than you. If you are a youth pastor, you interact with parents of your youth group members. If you are pastoring, you relate to people of all ages. Some young leaders find it challenging to work with those who are considerably older than them.

Here is how one twenty-four-year-old leader stated the challenge, "It is intimidating to face older people." Other young leaders would not say they are intimidated by older people, but they express some discomfort when working with the older crowd. A twenty-five-year-old music director said it this way:

> My greatest challenge is that everyone I lead is older than me. I enjoy bridging the gap. But it is not as easy as I thought it would be. I'm trying to appeal more to the conservative side. But I want to be who I am, too. It's like it is exciting versus traditional. I want to be more cutting edge and avante garde in my music. I'm trying to implement my passion, but not too much because I might offend those who are older. So, I'm trying to be middle of the road."

As a young leader, how are you to understand this challenge? I would place your challenges in at least three categories: style, perspective, and conviction.

First, your styles are generally different than those who are in their forties and older. Your preferences in music, clothes, and personal appearance (such as comfort with body piercings) probably range from slightly different to extremely different than those who are considerably older than you.

Second, your life perspective is different. You have recently moved into the adult work world whereas they have been engaged in that world for years and they now run it. You're probably more open to risk than they are. The nuances of political perspective probably differ. You're just starting out while some of them are nearing the end.

Third, the strength of your convictions differs. They have strong opinions about many things whereas you are forming opinions about many issues. They come on strong. They are convinced of their opinions about life in general, politics, and how a church should operate. To back up their opinions they give examples from past history using people and events that you haven't even heard of. It's easy to feel intimidated by them.

I could go on articulating the challenges of relating to older people because entire books have been written on this subject, but I've written enough to draw attention to the challenge and give some understanding of it.

What is a young leader to do? To put it into a phrase, lead and receive.

Lead and Receive

I think the best way to handle this challenge is to find a comfortable balance between being your own person while listening to others, including those older than you. You've got to both lead and receive.

On one hand, you've got to lead. If you are a youth pastor or lead pastor, you've got to lead your youth group or your church. You must have a vision, some strong convictions about where you want to take your youth group or church. If you always yield to the ideas of others you will not be seen as a leader. You've got to have backbone, some grit, and at times you need to dig in your heels and stand firm.

But on the other hand, you've got to receive from others, including those older than you. You must be open to the input of those older than you. They have a lot of experience. They are not always right, but you are wise to consider what they say.

How does this play out in a typical church? Let's say you are a youth pastor. As youth pastor you probably have people from the church helping you run the youth group. I'll call them youth sponsors, and they range in age from young to old. Those youth sponsors have ideas, sometimes very strong ideas, regarding how the youth work should be done. What often happens in this situation? How does the youth pastor respond? One unhealthy response is that the youth pastor abdicates leadership of the youth group to a specific sponsor or group of sponsors. Another unhealthy response is just the opposite, where the youth pastor won't listen to the ideas of the youth sponsors. The best response is when the youth pastor both leads and receives. The youth leader must be able to receive the sponsors' input into the youth ministry without surrendering the nonnegotiable values he holds dear. To put it another way: A leader must be strong, but must be a team leader who knows how to utilize all the gifts and experience that his team members bring to the task at hand. This is a challenge for all ministers, but particularly for young leaders.

Working with Volunteers

I remember reading about a businessman who sold his business and became an associate pastor. He said that one of the greatest challenges he faced as an associate pastor was working with volunteers. In fact, his opinion was that being in the ministry was much more difficult than leading a business, primarily due to the challenge of having to rely on a large number of volunteers.

Ministers face a unique challenge in the workplace—much of their work depends upon volunteers who can capriciously decide to quit their ministry and even the church. In the business world, an employee who quits faces loss of salary and medical benefits. But in the church world, volunteers who quit lose neither of those. Ministers must learn how to deal with their volunteers, whatever their level of maturity.

I asked one seventy-year-old pastor what advice he would give to a twenty-year-old minister, and he said, "Patience in dealing with people is a key; patience in dealing with people's lack of consistency and commitment. People today are busy, and for some church is not a priority. People have idiosyncrasies."

Patience is the name of the game when working with volunteers. I heard a pastor describe a church he visited while on vacation. Just minutes before the church service was to begin, he and his family were seated with the rest of the congregation while the pianist softly played worship choruses. The visiting pastor was enjoying the quiet, worshipful atmosphere. Just then the sound man emerged from the side of the stage with a cordless microphone in hand, walked on stage, and placed the mic in the stand. Then he tried to turn it on but was unsuccessful so he began pushing buttons, taking it apart, screwing it in tighter, all the while trying to get it working. While he was doing this, occasionally the mic would turn on and produce a loud squawk, then turn off, then turn on and produce another squawk. It was a noisy process. This happened several times until he finally got the mic to work. Meanwhile, the spirit of worship that had been evident before he emerged on stage was totally gone. The pastor reflected on this experience: "If only he had taken care of the microphones before the congregation had assembled, he would not have disrupted the great spirit of worship."

Any pastor knows most volunteers don't do this kind of thing deliberately. This guy didn't intentionally quench the spirit of worship that day. But he needed to be patiently taught and perhaps reminded of the best way to set up the microphones. Volunteers make mistakes, as we all do. Sometimes they show up a little too late, don't always know how to work with the church technology, and say things in a way that offends others. The young leader must recognize that patience is a key to effective relationships with volunteers.

Dealing with the Consumer Mentality

I was teaching a leadership workshop for ministers and asked them to fill out a survey that included the following question: *What is the greatest challenge you face?* One minister responded, "My anger at the consumer mentality in my church."

One of the challenges of ministry in the twenty-first century is the consumer mentality in churches. People are looking not for how they can serve in the local church, but what the church can do for them. And if they feel the church is not serving them well, they are ready to move on to another one, now.

Many of you in the ministry are surprised and dismayed by the consumer mentality that exists in the American church because you weren't raised with that mentality. When you were a teenager you were leaders in your church and youth group. You were service-oriented, not consumer-oriented. You were "on fire" for the Lord, sacrificing time and effort, working diligently as a volunteer alongside your youth pastor or pastor. When you became a minister you may have expected the people in your church or kids in your youth group to be as you once were, willing to work hard and sacrifice for the Lord. But it may be that now you are surprised and even disillusioned when you see the prevalence of the consumer mentality in churches and youth groups.

The Scriptures place a lot of emphasis on the value of gentle instruction. Young minister must learn the value of gently instructing those in their church or youth group. As 2 Timothy 2:24 says, "The Lord's servants must not quarrel but must be kind to everyone. They must be able to teach effectively and be patient with difficult people."

Paul warned Timothy about the consumer mentality that would exist in the Ephesus church: "For a time is coming when people will no longer listen to right teaching. They will follow their own desires and will look for teachers who will tell them whatever they want to hear. They will reject the truth and follow strange myths. But you should keep a clear mind in every situation. Don't be afraid of suffering for the Lord. Work at bringing others to Christ. Complete the ministry God has given you" (2 Tim. 4:3-5, NLT).

Roles Have Changed

You've heard of "sticker shock?" That's the astonished feeling within as you look at a sticker on the window and see the high cost of that automobile you want. You say, "Whoa, I didn't expect it to cost that much!" Similarly, as a young minister you may experience a "role shock" when you first enter the ministry.

How does this "role shock" occur? It happens as you move from being the target of ministry to being the leader in ministry. Your role changes. When you were a teenager in the church, or just after you received Christ as a young adult, you were the ministry target—the church pastors directed their efforts toward you. The pastors were trying to disciple you and would bend over backward to help you. The pastors and others would sacrifice for you. It was all about you.

But when you enter the ministry and take on a leadership role, the tables are turned. Others' expectations toward you change. You won't be pampered or coddled. At times, you will be the target of criticism and other talk surrounding your leadership. Formerly, you may have seen your pastor or youth pastor dealing with difficult people in the church, but most likely you didn't have to deal with those people. Now, you may have to deal directly with them. Once you were a spectator, now you are a participant, and perhaps even a mediator in conflict. The challenge is to realize that your role has changed, and to willingly and gladly accept that new role, and the challenges that accompany that change in role.

Responding to Criticism and Scrutiny in a Healthy Way

Later in this book I devote a full chapter to dealing with criticism, but I want to touch on it here because it is a major issue when discussing how to work with people.

One twenty-two-year-old minister, who had been in full-time ministry for only three years warned, "Watch out for criticism. When we are criticized and we take it personally, it tends to destroy our call so that we want to quit."

Our response to criticism, especially when we are young, is often similar to Moses' response. When he was criticized he wanted to quit. That seems to be a fairly normal response; some things never change.

In my conversations with young ministers, they say that they expect some criticism as church leaders, but criticism is difficult to take when it is unexpected and undeserved.

Unexpected criticism: I've found that criticism is almost always unexpected. Rarely do we drive to work expecting to be criticized. It hits us from the side, and we respond, "Whoa, I didn't see THAT coming." If we had seen it coming we could've prepared for it, perhaps.

Undeserved criticism: When we feel it's undeserved, it's particularly hard to swallow. Perhaps we have been criticized and feel that the criticizer has "no room to talk," that he has huge faults of his own. Or, perhaps we conclude that the "criticizer" doesn't know all the facts, or is seeing things from only one, limited perspective.

Years ago, while doing research for another project, I asked a number of leaders this question: "In ministry it is helpful to keep a soft heart but also develop a tough hide. How do we do this?" Think about it. It is difficult to do. Too often, when we try to develop a tough hide (meaning that we don't let criticism affect us), we close our inner selves to others and lose some of the sensitivity that facilitates relationships. But when we try to keep a soft heart, it seems inevitable that someone comes along and pierces it with words of criticism.

It is a challenge to have a soft heart but a tough hide. But it is possible. For the younger minister, two strategies seem especially helpful: First, when criticized, find a friend or mentor with whom you can share the criticisms. Try to find somebody with years of experience who has weathered criticism well. Releasing your thoughts to another will lessen your stress. Second, hang on to your intimacy with Christ. Stay close to Jesus. Let him soften your heart. The psalmist expressed his inner thoughts to God, and so should we. Taking both of these measures will help you receive criticism in a healthy manner and yet maintain a soft heart.

Responding to Criticism from Family or Those Close to You

A special kind of criticism occurs when the young minister is serving in a church where he or she grew up. One minister who is serving in the church where she grew up had this say: "Criticisms hurt. It's like salt in the wound because I grew up with these people. I have a desire to do my best. When I am criticized by someone I grew up with, that is almost as crippling as criticism coming from a family member. I've got to suck it up."

After talking about the specific criticisms toward her that unfortunately had been made public, this same minister concluded, "Being scrutinized is better when it is not so public. But I've grown from it. I've learned to be adaptable. I have a thicker skin now. I'm sensitive by nature. But I'm not letting things bother me as much."

Moses was criticized by his own relatives: Miriam and Aaron. Those who criticized him were close to him—those who had been some of his greatest supporters. Young leaders who grew up in the church where they are now working must be prepared to encounter criticism from people close to them, even from their relatives.

Selfish People

Consider the story of Lot and Abraham (Genesis 13:5-13). When they decided to settle down, Lot chose the best part of the land. It was a case of selfishness. Lot could have deferred to Abraham and let him choose which part of the land he wanted. But instead, Lot chose the best part of the land. Young ministers will find that they deal with people who, though claiming to be Christ followers, always seem to choose the best part for themselves.

This is an opportunity to model the forgiveness that is at the center of Christ's message. As leaders, God has given us the responsibility of modeling the behavior we want to see expressed in others. It is not easy, but the Spirit will enable us to forgive as Christ forgave.

Hebrews 12:24 tells us, "You have come to Jesus, the one who mediates the new covenant between God and people, and to the sprinkled blood, *which graciously forgives instead of crying out for vengeance as the blood of Abel did.*" (Italics added) Forgiveness is the way of God.

At times we want to cry out to God and urge Him to take vengeance for the way others have treated us: "Give em what they deserve, God. That'll teach em." I remember times as I was growing up when I deserved a lot worse than what I received, when I was given grace instead of justice.

When I was in junior high school, I was part of a youth group that mistreated our youth pastor. He was new to the church and he was not fitting in at all. He was unpopular with the youth and even with many of the parents, although I don't remember why. But some of the kids took their dislike of him way too far. One Sunday night after church they threw eggs at his front screen door and created a sick-looking mess on the screen and entry door. It must have taken a lot of time to clean up.

That's not the way to express your displeasure with the youth pastor. I didn't throw the eggs. I learned of the incident after the fact, but I should've said something in his defense. I should've stood up for the youth pastor, but I said nothing. Perhaps in his prayer times the youth pastor cried out to God for vengeance upon us; I doubt it. I remember that he was kind to us even after that incident. We didn't get what we deserved.

Another time, years after the egg incident, I was helping a different youth pastor move and he asked me to back his car and the U-haul trailer into the driveway. As I did so, I turned at too sharp an angle and the trailer placed a large dent into the side of the back left panel of the car. However, my youth pastor didn't ask me to pay for it; he never sent me a bill for the damages.

Neither experience qualifies as a particularly serious offense, but in those and many other situations I should have received some kind of punishment or discipline, but didn't. The youth pastors suffered some kind of loss, but they didn't require justice.

The kingdom of God is all about grace—the grace of God toward us and the grace that He calls us to extend to others. The selfish people we deal with test our willingness to extend grace, but when we do so we are being like Jesus, and that's one of the greatest goals we could attain in life.

Questions for Young Leaders

1. What kind of people do you have trouble getting along with?

2. What frustrating personal relationships are you experiencing?

3. Who do you go to for encouragement and refreshment?

4. Are people catching your vision? If not, are you blaming them? What should you do differently? How should you think differently?

5. What five words would you use to describe your relationship with older people in your ministry (examples: *enjoyable, intimidating, mentor-like, exasperating*)?

6. How do you normally respond to criticism?

Questions for Lead Pastors or Ministry Directors

1. Think of a young leader who works with you. Are people catching the young leader's ministry vision? If so, why? If not, why not?

2. How do your young leaders do in recruiting and working with volunteers?

3. When your young leaders are criticized, how do you protect and defend them?

Recommendations for Lead Pastors or Ministry Directors

1. Paul instructs Timothy to "Patiently correct, rebuke, and encourage your people with good teaching" (2 Timothy 4:2, NLT). Some would need correcting, some would need something stronger, such as a rebuke, and others would need encouraging. Our response should fit the need.

   Discuss with your young leaders...
   + when you should correct
   + when you should rebuke
   + when you should encourage

   Young leaders learn a lot from our personal experiences. Share as many as possible.

2. With your young leaders, brainstorm and list "Ten Commandments for Working with Volunteers." List the top three most difficult commandments to implement.

Challenge # 7

Challenges Related to Mentors

One forty-year-old minister stated, "I've had a lot of good people around me. I've kept in touch with four guys who have given me good advice on ministry questions and situations."

That minister was fortunate. He had four mentors. The challenge for many of those who are age twenty to thirty is finding helpful mentoring relationships.

One minister recalled a friend who had just quit the ministry: "I had a friend in ministry who was a youth pastor. He just quit the ministry because he and the lead pastor's wife had quarrels and disagreements. If he'd had a mentor, perhaps he'd still be in ministry today."

Mentors can make the difference between a minister quitting or persevering. Following are some of the ways a mentor can help a leader:

+ giving timely, encouraging advice
+ risking his or her own reputation in backing the leader
+ bridging between the leader and needed resources
+ modeling and setting expectations that challenge the leader
+ giving literary information that opens perspectives for the leader
+ giving financially, sometimes sacrificially, to further the leader's ministry
+ co-ministering in order to increase the credibility, status, and prestige of the leader
+ having the freedom to allow and even promote the leader beyond the mentor's own level of leadership.[25]

One leader referred to his mentor as his spiritual father: "I had a spiritual father, a pastor I admired. He had spiritual disciplines in his life, and he would tell me what I needed to hear and not just what I wanted to hear."

So what are the challenges facing young ministers who are looking for, and communicating with, mentors?

It's Easier Said Than Done

Though people are talking a lot these days about the value of mentoring and coaching, I still hear young ministers say that they find it difficult to find and develop a worthwhile mentoring relationship.

A leader of youth pastors said it this way: "Back in my day of youth pastoring, it (mentoring) wasn't happening. It is getting better now. The young guys would still like to be mentored. They really yearn for that, but they don't get it a lot."

The Natural Choice May Not Work

It would seem natural that young leaders would look to their immediate situation for mentoring. One youth leader said that many youth pastors want to be mentored by the lead pastors with whom they work.

When I was in my twenties I was a youth pastor in two churches. In one of those situations, my lead pastor and I sat in his living room numerous times and just talked about ministry with no set agenda. A lot of our conversation centered on the church where we were both employed. It was relaxed and unplanned. It was a valuable time.

However, I've learned that there is great variety in the experiences of young ministers and their relationships with their lead pastors. One minister who trains youth leaders said this:

> Most lead pastors do not value mentoring—they don't value being a Moses to Joshua. I get surprised by pastors, many of whom are very relational, but they aren't mentoring. They aren't even doing what we might call level-one mentoring, that is, just casually talking about ministry

with the young guys, recommending a book from time to time, or discussing the challenges that the young guys are facing. But the young guys want to be mentored.

One lead pastor told me flat out that he was not interested in mentoring his youth pastor. He said that he hired his youth pastor to do a job and expected it to be done with very little or no coaching from him as the lead pastor. I imagine there are a number of lead pastors who feel that way.

And then there are lead pastors who would like to mentor their youth pastors but just can't find the time to do it. Life is busy, and there is rarely enough time to do all you want to do.

(It should be noted, too, that some lead pastors would like to mentor their youth pastor but the youth pastor is not interested, for whatever reason.)

So we have some, perhaps many, young ministers who want mentoring from their lead pastors. But we have lead pastors who don't want to or don't plan to mentor them. That is a challenge. So, as a young minister, realize that your best bet for finding mentoring may or may not come from the most natural source, your lead pastor.

Consider these ideas for finding a good mentor:

+ Evaluate your present relationships and ask who you feel comfortable talking to about everyday matters. That level of comfort affords a good foundation for a mentoring relationship.

+ Ask your friends who has helped them.

+ Ask the leaders of your minister's association or denomination who they'd recommend as a mentor.

+ Some mentoring relationships are set up not to address specific leadership skills, but to discuss your current challenges. Look for someone who listens well to you.

+ For those mentoring relationships where you want to develop leadership skills, identify specific skills or capacities that you need to develop, and look around for mentors who can mentor you in those specific skills. Avoid setting your sights too high and looking for a mentor who does everything well. I don't know if there is such a person, but it is better to define specifically what you are looking for and find somebody who does that one thing well. For example, if you find that you lack team leader skills, find someone who does that well and ask him to meet with you once a month for three months, and discuss that specific skill.

Finding a Mentor for the Minister's Wife

Sometimes male ministers forget that their wives also want, and need, a mentor. I talked to several young ministers who talked about the difficulty their wives were having in finding their own mentors.

One associate pastor, speaking of his wife, said it this way:

> In her first five years of ministry, my wife really struggled. She didn't realize what she had signed up for. She worked full time in the corporate world and was assisting me in my work as associate pastor. She didn't have anyone she felt she could go to with her questions and problems. She went a few times to our lead pastor's wife, but it just didn't go well. The lead pastor's wife would just tell her to deal with it and get with it.

Don't underestimate the value of helping your wife finding a mentor. As I've progressed through the years of ministry I've seen a number of Christian leaders who were hindered in their ministry primarily due to the lack of ministry development in their wives. Other minister wives totally derailed from ministry, which placed their husbands in difficult situations.

Developing an Effective Mentor Relationship

Some young ministers have participated in mentoring programs but have not found it helpful. One young leader reflected on his days at a Christian university that had instituted a mentor program for the ministerial students. He expressed disappointment in his mentor relationship: "[My college] provided internships. I was involved in two of them. I was assigned a mentor but we just sat in his office and talked."

I don't know what the young leader was expecting in the mentoring relationship, but whatever it was, he didn't get it. So, the challenge for some is finding a mentor relationship that provides sufficient support, or training, or whatever it is he feels he needs.

Think about these tips for developing an effective relationship with a mentor:

+ Realize that you may have to be the primary driver and agenda setter of your mentor relationship, particularly if your mentor is offering this service to you free of charge.

+ If you initiate the mentoring relationship, be clear as to what you are expecting. A common concern I hear is that the leader wants someone with whom he can process the challenges he is facing. The focus is on discussing issues that the leader is facing. Avoid saying that you want to tap the leader's expertise. Many leaders don't feel like experts and shy away from relationships with such high expectations.

+ Come prepared with specific questions.

+ Learn to draw out the wisdom and knowledge of your mentor with good follow-up questions. If is often the question after the initial question which yields valuable insight.

+ Realize that you will not agree with your mentor on some of his/her recommendations.

+ Build a relationship with your mentor before disagreeing with him in your meetings. Meet with your mentor several times before you venture to disagree with him or her.

Mentors Who Disappoint

One leader, age sixty-four, reflected on his early years of ministry.

On the positive side, I had some good mentors. They made a great impact on me! But on the negative side, some of my mentors were very flawed individuals. They had their own demons that they were wrestling with. So, one of my challenges was dealing with the disappointing mentors.

Other leaders can attest to the profound disappointment that results from developing a genuine and seemingly transparent relationship with an older leader only to see him confess later on to long-standing sins in his own life. Choose your mentors carefully, but realize that some will not live up to expectations.

Don't Lose Hope

Though the previous pages contain quotes of young leaders who were not receiving the mentoring they craved from their leaders, many have been deeply satisfied with the mentoring they received. So, if you want to develop a mentoring relationship with your lead pastor or the leader of your ministry, don't lose hope. Try to develop the relationship. It may turn out to be a source of great strength and encouragement.

Lead pastors and other leaders are busy. So, if you want to develop a mentoring relationship, you may need to initiate it and persevere in developing it. I spoke with a single, twenty-nine-year-old leader—I'll call him Mike—who reflected on his experiences as a part-time staff member at a church in the Northwest. Mike recalled a mentoring relationship with his lead pastor that provided valuable direction in his life. It was a mentoring relationship that Mike had initiated.

Mike referred to himself as a "watcher." He watched his lead pastor and how he lived his life. He noticed how his pastor's kids—especially his boys—idolized him, like a hero. So Mike approached his pastor and asked, "Can we meet? Will you mentor me?" Mike initiated the relationship and they began meeting.

I asked Mike what was most valuable about the mentoring relationship and he replied:

My pastor told me that he felt impressed by God to share with me one thing in particular—the value of consistency. I didn't know what he meant by that. So, my pastor said, "How often do you pray for [the person who will be] your future wife?" I said, 'Not much.' He urged, "Do it, consistently."

So Mike wrote a prayer for his future wife and placed it in his Bible as a bookmark to help him remember to pray for her. He prays consistently for her. He had obviously taken his pastor's lesson to heart.

Mike's story is an illustration of how a mentoring relationship with a lead pastor can develop and work. Notice that the information the lead pastor shared was not earth-shattering. It was a simple lesson that the lead pastor had learned and then passed on to Mike. The value of the mentoring relationship is in both the content and the relationship. First, good content is shared. In Mike's case, it was the importance of consistency. Second, and perhaps more significantly, is that a meaningful relationship is established between the mentor and leader. Leaders of all ages need those kinds of relationships if they are to endure in the ministry.

Questions for Young Leaders

1. If you have a mentor, what three qualities does the mentor have that make your relationship with him/her enjoyable and helpful?

2. If you had a master mentor sitting with you right now, what advice would you ask for?

3. What leadership skills do you most need to develop? List them below:

   Skill #1 _____

   Skill #2 _____

   Skill #3 _____

Now, think of a leader you know who excels at skill #1, and put his/her name next to that skill. Consider asking that leader to meet with you once for fifteen minutes so you might ask him/her, "What would you recommend I do to improve in this leadership skill?"

Do the same for skills #2 and #3.

Questions for Lead Pastors or Ministry Directors

1. Who have been your mentors? What did each provide?

2. What makes a mentor relationship work? What damages or destroys a mentor relationship?

3. If a young leader wanted to develop a mentor relationship with you, would you be willing to mentor him/her, and if so, what parameters would you set to make the mentor relationship effective? For example, how often would you want to meet and for how long?

Recommendations for Lead Pastors or Ministry Directors

1. Encourage your young leaders to develop mentor relationships. If you can provide mentoring, let them know. If not, let them know that too, and recommend someone who is available to provide mentoring.

2. Share with young leaders how you have been helped by mentors.

3. Provide "tips" for young leaders who want to develop mentoring relationships. For example, share with them, "If you want to develop mentoring relationships with other ministers, here is how I'd recommend you go about it..."

Challenge # 8

Dealing with Criticism

A lot of us receive sermon illustrations and stories via email every day. Some I save, and others I delete. Here's a favorite:

> Mildred, the church gossip and self-appointed arbiter of the church's morals kept sticking her nose into other people's business. Several members were unappreciative of her activities, but feared her enough to maintain their silence. She made a mistake, however, when she accused George, a new member, of being an alcoholic after she saw his pickup truck parked in front of the town's only bar one afternoon. She commented to George and others that everyone who had seen it there would surely know what he was doing!!
>
> George, a man of few words, stared at her for a moment and just walked away. He didn't explain, defend, or deny, he said nothing.
>
> Later that evening, George quietly parked his pickup in front of Mildred's house ... and left it there... ALL NIGHT LONG!!!

I like that story because George obtained a measure of justice. He was able to give an effective response to criticism, and he did it without saying a word. I wish that all of us could silence our critics that easily. But we can't.

I looked up the word *criticism* in word search and the first synonyms listed were *censure, disapproval, disparagement, condemnation,* and *denigration.* The word *criticism* sounds kind of harmless compared to the sound of several of those synonyms. But make no mistake about it, criticism can be a dangerous weapon.

Paul wrote in Ephes. 6:16 "In every battle you will need faith as your shield to stop the fiery arrows aimed at you by Satan."

Some of the criticism we receive is just that, a fiery dart aimed to destroy us.

Criticism is tough to take, particularly when you are just starting out in ministry. Our reactions to criticism vary from mild to severe. When the criticizer has little respect among others, it is easy to discount his or her criticism, and our response is fairly mild. But when the person who criticizes us is well-respected our response can be severe. Criticism is often a visceral issue—when we are criticized we get tense, our stomach tightens, and often it's difficult to respond to the criticizer rationally.

We all know that we should listen to the criticism and, if justified, change our behavior. As someone said, criticism should make us better, not bitter. We know that. But I realize that no matter how many sound principles I give for dealing with criticism, once you actually face your first major dose of criticism in the ministry, it's still difficult to take. I hope this chapter helps you sort through the criticism you receive in ministry.

Shell-Shocked

Do you remember the opening scene in the movie, "Saving Private Ryan?" In that scene, the allied forces were attacking the Nazis on D-Day in Northern France and the Germans' artillery fire was so intense that many allied soldiers were jarred into a state of "shell-shock." They were disoriented and temporarily deafened. They hunkered down behind barriers instead of moving forward. In that state they were immobilized, unable to mount an immediate and significant counterattack.

As a young minister, you can find yourself in a similar state. You've taken on your first ministry experience—you have entered into full spiritual combat, intense criticism has come your way, and you feel assaulted. You feel emotionally shocked. Criticism can upset your identity and security. You may have a reaction similar to shell-shock: You're confused and unable to move forward.

When those early and unexpected criticisms come your way, it is common to have reactions such as, "I didn't see that coming," or "How was I supposed to know that?" You entered full-time ministry hoping to help people find purpose in life and then, wham, you are hit with a barrage of criticism.

I've used the war analogy as I've talked about criticism, but this analogy breaks down at a certain point because, though soldiers know the barrage is coming, it doesn't prevent being shell-shocked. But I'm convinced that if young ministers are aware that criticism is coming they can prevent this feeling of shell-shock and the immobilization that follows.

Criticism accompanies leadership. It comes with the territory. All who are in leadership will be criticized. Expect it. If you are not criticized at least occasionally, pinch yourself and ask, "Am I really alive? Am I breathing? Am I leading?" I've found that if you arm yourself with this expectation, you will not be "shell-shocked" when it happens.

By expecting criticism, I am not encouraging you to live in fear, but just with a quiet understanding that you will, with God's help, withstand and overcome the negative attitudes of some people.

Seeing Criticism as Your Friend

I played basketball and football in high school and college, so I sat under the teaching of a number of coaches. One line that several of those coaches gave me during practice sessions was always hard to swallow. They would say something like this: "Ben, don't mind it when I criticize you. That just means that I think you're worth criticizing, that I want you to do better, and that you are valuable to this team. Be concerned when I don't criticize your play; that means that you no longer fit into my plans on this team and that I don't care if you improve." Those were not the exact words, but several coaches stated that same principle. That message was easy to forget when the coach was screaming at me and slapping my helmet. But those coaches had a point.

Criticism really is one of your best friends.

Proverbs 25:12 says, "Valid criticism is as treasured by the one who heeds it as jewelry made from finest gold." (NLT)

The problem is that criticism can be so tough to take. It seems to assault my very identity, telling me that I'm no good, that I won't make it, and that I should get away from the criticizer. But, in reality, if the criticism has any basis in truth, and if it is received well, it is setting me up for improvement and success.

My coaches' words mirror what the writer of Hebrews says in 12:8: "If God doesn't discipline you as he does all of his children, it means that you are illegitimate and are not really his children after all." (NLT)

Discipline is not the same as criticism but both discipline and criticism can be signs of others' love and concern for you.

Losing Your Focus

Years ago, while traveling with a singing group in Kenya, I had the opportunity to be part of an African photo safari in the Masai Mara game reserve. It was one of the most interesting two days of my life. On the second day of the safari, we were up early and traveled in our bus to a river bank. As we stepped out of the bus, we saw what we had been searching for. There in front of us were several hippos wallowing in the river. But to our right, there was an unexpected and incredible sight. Two large elephants were feeding on the trees only thirty-five yards away.

It was about 7 AM, the air was crisp and there was a slight fog. The scene was like one from National Geographic. I'll never forget it. I was transfixed, taking pictures of the hippos and then of the elephants. Our group of twenty had hired a Kenyan armed guard to accompany us, and he had his rifle ready in case the elephants were spooked and charged us. We had been told to be very quiet and not upset the elephants. "If they turn toward us, that is not good. And watch their ears," the guard said, "if they spread out, get back in the bus, fast." Because I'd been looking up at the animals I didn't realize that I was standing on an anthill. Suddenly, I felt ants crawling up my leg, to my knees and even my thighs. Looking down at the anthill I saw that these were large ants. Then they began biting my legs. I started to jump up and down while swatting my legs to get them off me, making quite a commotion. You can imagine the reaction of the others, including the guard. "Shhh!" "You're gonna get us killed."

"Stop jumping, Ben!" I was aware of the danger from the elephants, but I couldn't help myself—my immediate concern was getting rid of the biting ants. Fortunately, after swatting the ants and then moving off the anthill, I calmed down and the elephants didn't charge us.

Have you ever lost your focus due to some distraction? That day in Africa, I lost my focus on two of the largest African animals because of one of the smallest.

Hebrews 12:2 tells us to fix our eyes on Jesus, the author and finisher of our faith. Criticism can cause you to lose your focus and instead turn it to one of two other sources. First, criticism can cause you to focus on you. When we are criticized it is easy to focus on protecting ourselves and our identities instead of focusing on God and His call on our life.

Taking criticism personally is easy to do. Criticism can push you to escape your commitments and ask, "Do I have what it takes to be a minister?" or "Is the ministry worth all of this garbage (criticism)?"

I have a hilarious DVD titled, "It's All about Me." In it the singer takes all the songs we normally sing to God and inserts "me." Instead of "How Great Thou Art" he sings "How Great I Am." Instead of "Oh, Come Let Us Adore Him" it is "Oh, Come Let Us Adore Me." That is what criticism can do. It can cause life to be all about me instead of Him and what He has called us to do.

Second, criticism can cause you to focus on your criticizer. Taking your eyes off Jesus and focusing on your criticizer is easy to do. You may fume internally about the criticism he leveled against you. You may talk to others about the criticizer and the unjust criticism he gave you. You might even meet the criticizer in a face-to-face confrontation.

Consider Nehemiah. When he was rebuilding the walls of Jerusalem, his enemies attacked his character. They attacked him personally with rumors (Neh. 6:6), deceit (Neh. 6:10-13), and false reports (Neh. 6:17). It would've been easy for Nehemiah to focus on himself and his ability to fulfill the call of God on his life. Or, Nehemiah could have spent his time focused on his enemies and combating what they were saying. Instead, Nehemiah kept his focus on God's call on his life.

> But I realized they were plotting to harm me, so I replied by sending this message to them: "I am doing a great work! I cannot stop to come and meet with you. (Neh. 6:3, NLT)

Take his response as your response: "I am doing a great work here at my church or in this ministry!" You are not doing just a good one—you are doing a great one! Think of it: Your work will result in people making decisions to spend eternity with Christ. Those decisions last forever. Never forget the importance of your work. Don't allow personal attacks to turn you away from your calling as a minister of the gospel.

I learned the value of this lesson watching a basketball game. The high scoring guard on one team was really talented. He had a great shot, and he knew how to drive to the basket and put his body in such a position that he was often fouled by the player guarding him. But it was evident that he also had a temper. And when players on the opposing team realized that, they did whatever they could to tick him off. From my position near the court, I could hear them calling him names, and I saw them hacking him and even punching him in the side so that he would get angry, lose his poise, and get out of control emotionally. And they were successful—that player lost his self-control. Once that happened, he lost his focus on the game and scoring, and his focus instead turned to personal battles with specific players on the opposing team. His anger eventually nullified his ability as a scorer because he found himself sitting on the bench to regain his composure.

Nehemiah did just the opposite. When criticized, he focused his attention on his great task, "I am doing a great work...I cannot come down." Be conscious of criticism and how it is affecting you. Responding to criticism properly will help preserve your calling.

Criticism and Its Effect on Your Spouse

When you are criticized, it is not only your identity that may be under assault, your spouse's identity may also be under assault. And, in turn, when your spouse is criticized, you, too, may feel that you have been criticized.

I have noticed through the years that when a guy in the ministry is criticized, his wife often "feels" that same criticism. In fact, sometimes her reaction to the criticism is more severe than that of her husband. Occasionally, I have seen a minister's wife who seemed just about ready to "take up arms" in defense of her husband. Those in the ministry must remember that it's not just us being attacked, but also our spouses.

Realizing this will help us see more acutely the necessity of a godly and courageous response to criticism, for we realize that we are models to our spouse and family of the godly way to react to criticism.

When Others Criticize Your Friends and Colleagues

I have been talking about the times when others criticize us, but one of the challenges for young ministers occurs when someone comes to you and criticizes someone else. For example, a church member may come to you and criticize a fellow staff member. In those cases, you have a number of options:

- You can politely end the conversation and leave.
- You can stay and be silent.
- You can stay and change the topic of the conversation.
- You can voice your discomfort and say something positive about the person being criticized.

One of my favorite books in the Bible is Proverbs, a practical book about life. The writer of Proverbs has a lot to say about our relationships with one another.

Proverbs 19:22 (NLT) states, "Loyalty makes a person attractive." One of the ways to demonstrate your loyalty to others is by not listening when others criticize your friends and colleagues, or even by rebuking the criticizer. Another relevant Proverb 20:6 (NLT): "Many will say they are loyal friends, but who can find one who is really faithful?"

Or, consider a slightly different situation. Suppose someone comes to you and criticizes your friend, and you realize that the person has a point, the criticism is justified. It is tempting to agree with the person. But you dare not encourage the criticizer. The book of Proverbs has a lot of great wisdom and one proverb applies specifically to this kind of situation. Proverbs 17:9 (NLT) says, "Disregarding another person's faults preserves love; telling about them separates close friends." In this situation it may be wise to voice your discomfort with the criticism and say something positive about your friend. By doing so you are sending the criticizer a message: "I'm loyal to my friends and colleagues."

And if nothing else, a great way to respond to criticism is to just simply say nothing, as Proverbs 17:28 (NLT) says: "Even fools are thought to be wise when they keep silent; when they keep their mouths shut, they seem intelligent." Say nothing in response to the criticism; then change the subject. They'll think you are wise (which I'm sure you are).

Lack of a Solid Foundation

On the Florida coast when a hurricane approaches residents board up the windows of their stores and houses. They know that if they prepare well, they can lessen the damage of the approaching storm. A storm is easier to survive if you're well prepared for it.

Young ministers should prepare today for the difficulties ahead! Experience and the Scriptures tell us that you will face trials in the future. It's wise to do all you can now to prepare for them. Remember that in the biblical parable the winds came and blew against the house, but it stood because it had a firm foundation. So, how is your foundation? Every day you are building some kind of foundation. Here are some common components of a firm foundation:

Supportive Relationships:
It's much easier to take criticism if you have affirming relationships in your life. Build solid relationships with your spouse and with others you interact with regularly. You will find great strength in these relationships when the trials come.

Mentors:
Mentors are different from the supportive relationships mentioned above. In this context, mentors are those who have knowledge and experience in the work you are doing. A friend or spouse offers a supportive relationship, but he or she may not be able to offer much helpful advice regarding your work. When things are going well, before the storms of ministry occur, cultivate relationships with people who have experience in your line of work. Then, when the trials come, if you need work-related advice you know where to find it, and others will be prepared to give it.

Why is mentoring of young leaders not occurring as much as hoped? The main reason normally given for the lack of mentoring is a lack of time, both on the part of the mentor and the leader. But leaders who do not pursue mentoring relationships with mentors pass up a powerful tool.

Speaking not of mentoring, but of coaching, a skill related to mentoring, one author had this say: "In short, the coaching [leadership] style may not scream 'bottom-line results,' but, in a surprisingly indirect way, it delivers them."[26] I agree. Coaching and mentoring help a leader produce results.

Preparation and Internships

Some who are reading this book are still in college and have not yet moved into full-time ministry. I urge you to take advantage of opportunities for internships. One benefit of an internship is that the intern can make some mistakes and learn from them before he or she jumps into a permanent position.

In the late 1990s I was staying in an apartment building in Southern Florida when a powerful hurricane swept through our area. But the apartment handyman had done such a good job of boarding and taping windows, the apartments were not damaged. In fact, he had done such a good job that I actually slept through the hurricane as it passed by at 3:00 A.M. I learned about the hurricane by reading the newspaper the next morning. Now that demonstrates good preparation (and a deep-sleeper). You will weather (pardon the pun) criticism better if you have prepared well by building into your life elements of a solid foundation.

Emotionally Closing Up Due to Criticism

Ministers often counsel people who are in tough situations. For example, when I was in my early twenties I ministered to young people in my youth group who were dealing with suicidal thoughts and family breakups. I found that when I would counsel them with gentleness and compassion they were generally responsive to my words. To effectively counsel and comfort people in crisis we must communicate a certain amount of gentleness and compassion. But one temptation we face when we are criticized, particularly it if is long-term criticism, is to emotionally close ourselves off to others. In response to criticism we can become so hardened that we find it difficult to demonstrate the compassion of Christ toward others.

The solution is to somehow be tough and tender, to toughen up but not close up.

We will be criticized, so we must have a tough hide. But we must not lose a tender heart. By toughening up, I mean that we must not let criticism overcome us. We cannot let it cause us to quit. We cannot let it get into our heart so that we become bitter. We must guard against allowing the criticism to take root and then developing an attitude toward others that is not constructive.

But by toughening up, I do not mean that we become stoic, or that we put on a hard exterior, or that we lose the compassion of Christ.

You have probably met people who've faced tough circumstances and have become hard and cold. In contrast, others have experienced circumstances just as difficult but continue to have warm and compassionate hearts. We can't control what happens to us but how we respond to our circumstances is up to us.

How do we toughen up without closing up? Several years ago I interviewed a number of ministers, asking that specific question (I referred to this in an earlier chapter, too). I was intrigued by their answers. Every minister I interviewed acknowledged the need to be tough without closing up but nobody could provide a step-by-step answer to that question as they often did in response to other questions I posed. The best solution that the ministers gave was to simply "stay close to Jesus." Staying close to Jesus had everything to do with cultivating one's relationship to Christ through the spiritual disciplines, primarily through prayer and times of reflection on the Word of God.

As I thought about their responses I realized that they were correct. The way to be both tough and tender is not to follow a five-point, step-by-step set of instructions. The best way is to build a close relationship with Jesus! That answer fits our life-situations. The Christ-follower walk has at its foundation a personal relationship with Christ, the idea that He is the vine and we are the branches and that if we abide in Him we have all the power we need, even the power to toughen up and yet not close up.

Questions for Young Leaders

1. Think of ways others—including parents, siblings, and teachers—criticized you as you grew up. How has the way

you were criticized then affected your involuntary and initial response to criticism today?

2. If a 19-year-old youth intern came to you and asked you for advice regarding how to handle criticism just leveled at him or her, what advice would you give? What would you tell him/her to do, and not do?

3. What prevents us from receiving and learning from criticism?

4. Like Nehemiah, who thought he was doing a great work, do you think you are doing a great work? List the reasons you think your work is a great work?

5. How does your spouse handle it when people criticize you?

6. How does a minister develop a soft heart and a tough hide?

Questions for Lead Pastors or Ministry Directors

1. How do the young leaders who work with you handle criticism?

2. What can you do to help them handle criticism better?

3. Think of a young leader who works with you. Is there a criticism that has been consistently leveled at him or her that has merit? How has the young leader reacted? As the young leader's boss how can you help the young leader react to the criticism in a healthy way?

Recommendations for Lead Pastors or Ministry Directors

1. Role play in staff meetings the following situations:

   • Someone comes to you, the youth pastor, and criticizes your lead pastor. What is your response?

- Someone comes to you and criticizes you to your face. What is your response?

- Someone comes to you and tells you of a third party who is spreading lies about you in the church or ministry. What do you say to the person who tells you this? What do you do about the third party?

2. Share with your young leaders your insights regarding how a minister can develop both a tough hide and a kind heart.

Ministry, Marriage, and Family Challenges

Challenge # 9

Balancing Ministry and Family

Twenty-four/seven is a term that is used today to describe something that happens all the time. Young ministers usually enter the ministry with great zeal, knowing that their work will result in eternal decisions by others. They are intensely dedicated to their task and many don't even think about the concept of "working overtime." They will work ten or twelve hours a day for little pay because they are committed to Jesus Christ and His message. They understand that full-time ministry is a twenty-four/seven kind of vocation.

If a young minister is single then such a schedule may be possible. It may not be wise but sometimes single guys or gals find it possible to work incredibly long hours. But for those who are married, and particularly if they are married with kids, working excessively long hours can create marriage and family problems.

An experienced minister reflected on his early years in ministry:

> I'm sort of a driven person, a motivated person. I was very motivated in my work, and had the tendency early on to spend little time with my family. We had one car, and our first baby arrived. I realized that I needed to switch gears now that I'm a dad. I think my wife was suffering from postpartum depression, and with having

103

only one car (that I was using), she felt confined. *She was ready to go live with her parents again* (emphasis mine). So I had to learn how to balance family and ministry.

This minister's wife was ready to leave him. That simple sentence is easy to miss, and that is why I italicized it. We expect that the long work hours will help our ministry or church but often it hurts our marriages and families, and therefore, in the long run, may hurt our ministry. Knowing that long hours can place a strain on a marriage and family, one lead pastor requires his staff members to spend four nights a week at home with their families, not at the church. Perhaps other pastors should do the same with their staff members.

This balance between work and family is important. When we relegate our marriages to a place of lesser importance, we risk failure. Being in ministry is different from many occupations. Being divorced doesn't affect a plumber's work. When you call the plumber your top concern isn't whether he is married or divorced, your immediate concern is that he does good work for a good price. But, for a minister, divorce can create an obstacle to ministry. Don't get me wrong, I know of a number of divorced ministers who have solid ministries, but the fact of the divorce usually has not helped their ministry. Instead, the divorce has created obstacles for their ministry. The lesson? Find the proper balance between work and family.

What are the specific challenges related to the balance between ministry and family?

Understanding the Importance of Balancing Ministry and Family

A fifty-six-year-old minister talked about this issue:

A challenge is that you've got to protect your family. We talk about our priorities, that God must be first, family is second, and ministry is third, but we [referring to those in his generation] modeled God first, ministry second, and family third. When you put your family ahead of ministry, others accuse you of being a slacker. But there have been plenty of guys who didn't make it in ministry because they had not been balanced, and, as a result, their wives were depressed. The ministers' wives and kids became sour toward ministry and God. It is hard to sweeten them up once they've been soured on God and ministry.

Recently I was talking with a leader I'll call Greg, who reflected on a life-changing experience he had. He said he was part of an audience that was listening to a well-known, older minister who had been used by God to start two major ministries that are still successful today. The well-known minister said, "I sacrificed my family for God." Greg was incensed at the minister's words: "It was like he was boasting about sacrificing his family for God. He said it in a proud way." Greg continued, "But later on in his talk, this minister went on to admit, 'My kids don't live for God.'"

Many ministers have sacrificed their families for their ministries. The ministers' kids have turned away from the church and God because of the misplaced priorities of their fathers. I have no desire to heap condemnation on them. Most of them feel very sorry for their misplaced priorities, and some continue to struggle with guilt over this issue.

There are several reasons to get these priorities correct:

First, your marriage and family will be healthier. Spouses and kids want to spend time together as a family. As someone has said, in families love is spelled "time."

Second, you will be modeling good behavior for your kids. The values of the parents are unconsciously passed down to the kids. More is caught than taught.

Third, you will be modeling good behavior for those in your ministry. Young leaders are models to others in their youth group or ministries. What are you modeling for your people? What are you modeling for your staff members? They may follow your example.

One minister explained it this way: "Some ministers are so busy that their spouses have great resentment and anger toward the church. And, for some youth and associate pastors, their spouses are angry at the lead pastor because he is modeling unhealthy behavior toward their husbands." Being a poor model reverberates throughout the ministry.

Forces that Throw Off the Family and Work Balance

In later paragraphs I will write about the egocentric forces that fuel our dysfunctions and how they damage our balance. But some of the forces that throw off our balance are good forces, such as a solid work ethic and a desire to please Christ.

A solid work ethic is a good thing. It is one of the values that has fueled the success of the United States, and of course, many other countries. That work ethic has provided a well-constructed house on a solid foundation that I can live in and not worry that the roof will cave in at any moment. That ethic has provided a car that I can drive all the way to New York and back with few or no problems. That work ethic allows me to board planes without worrying about whether the mechanics have checked them out and whether they are safe. A solid work ethic is too often undervalued.

But the solid work ethic, if taken too far, can damage our family relationships.

Another good force is the desire to please Christ. Those of us in the ministry often work long hours out of gratitude for what Jesus Christ has done for us. But we can overdo it, causing our laudable motivation of gratitude toward Christ to work against our family health.

Those are just two of the positive forces that can be misapplied and therefore work against our work/family balance. Let's consider several of the negative forces that work against this balance.

I believe that sometimes we don't take into account the powerful forces of ego and identity and how they influence this work/marriage/family balance. For example, sometimes our need to look good in the eyes of others, or look better than a colleague, is what is actually driving our schedule and priorities. We may not acknowledge those egocentric drives because it is so easy in ministry to attribute our busy schedule to "doing the Lord's work." But if we stop long enough to examine why we keep the long hours and neglect our family we may discover that our motives are not always as pure as we think.

Two authors who have written about these motives and egocentric drives are McIntosh and Rima, in their book, *Overcoming the Dark Side of Ministry*. They refer to improper motives as *the dark side*:

"The dark side, though sounding quite sinister, is actually a natural result of human development. It is the inner urges, compulsions, and dysfunctions of our personality that often go unexamined or remain unknown to us until we experience an emotional explosion or some other significant problem that causes us to search for a reason why. Because it is a part of us that we are unaware of to some degree, lurking in the shadows of our personality, we have labeled it the dark side of our personality."[27]

All of these words: *the dark side, sinister, lurking, shadows*—they all sound like something out of the Star Wars world. But McIntosh and Rima go on to describe how the "dark side" contributes not only to things that undermine us, but also how the dark side contributes to our successes: "However, in spite of the foreboding mental image the term *dark side* creates, it is not, exclusively a negative force in our lives. In almost every case the *factors* that eventually undermine us are shadows of the ones that contribute to our success."[28]

What kinds of factors are they (and I) referring to? They would include such forces as personal insecurities, inferiority feelings, and the need for parental approval. These and many other dysfunctions are sometimes the forces that compel us to become imbalanced in our schedule and to neglect our families. These dysfunctions are often the ones that cause leaders to become successful but they are very often the same issues that lead to their failure.

McIntosh and Rima assert the following assumptions:

1. Every leader suffers from some degree of personal dysfunction, varying from extremely mild to extremely acute.

2. Personal dysfunction, in one form or another, can often serve as the driving force behind an individual's desire to achieve success as a leader.

3. Many leaders are not aware of the dark side of their personalities and the personal dysfunctions that drive them.

4. Learning about their own dark side and the dysfunctions that have created it can enable leaders to address those areas and prevent, or at least mitigate the potential negative effects to their exercise of leadership.[29]

The best leaders learn to pair the two capacities of self-awareness and honesty. I want to do so. I would encourage you to become more aware of the driving forces behind your desire to achieve success. If, in the discovery process, you learn of impure motives and forces, honestly face them and ask God to help you overcome them.

Specific Issues

As you reflect on your family/work balance, consider the four questions below. I hope that these questions provide further clarification regarding how to achieve a healthy family/work balance.

First: When you signed on to your present ministry what was your employment agreement regarding time and schedule? This agreement would include both what was written into your job contract and whatever was verbally agreed upon between you and your boss. More simply put, what are the expectations that your lead pastor or boss has of you? What does the official board expect? You have an obligation to live up to the original agreements, as does your boss.

Second: Do you take a day off each week? I've heard some ministers brag that they never take a day off. But, over the years, I've also concluded that the ones who survive in the long haul are those who take a day off each week. Taking a day off is biblical (the Sabbath) and it is wise. There are times when a day off is not possible because of the need to do a funeral or some other unexpected commitment, but generally, it should be a weekly day off.

Third: Is the young minister's spouse expected to attend all church meetings? This is a huge issue for young ministers, particularly in this day when many of the young ministers' spouses are working full-time outside the church or ministry. The issue is not whether the spouse will attend the Sunday morning service. Normally, that is not a problem. The issue is whether the spouse will attend other meetings at the church. This is a matter that you should discuss specifically with your spouse and boss.

Some lead pastors expect to get two for the price of one. Every minister who has been around for a while knows what that means. The young minister is hired but the expectation is that the spouse will work almost full time in the church, too, but without pay. This expectation is not as common as it once was.

I've seen plenty of conflict on this issue, and many involve the question of what church meetings the spouse should or should not attend. In my mind I picture the conflict like this: The lead pastor is pulling the arm of the young minister one direction, while the young minister's spouse and children are pulling the minister's other arm in the other direction, and the young minister is in the middle trying to keep himself from being torn apart.

The best time to resolve this issue is before you take the position at the church or ministry. Ask about your boss's expectations toward your spouse. And then decide, in collaboration with your spouse, if you can live with those expectations.

If this issue was not discussed before you were hired but conflicts arise in this area later, it will require some frank discussion, and probably some give and take. Hopefully, your boss will do some of the giving.

Fourth: Are the "seasons of life" given consideration? When I took a youth pastor position in the summer of 1983, I was single. I was able to work long hours at the church. I actually lost ten pounds in a month because I was so involved in my work that I often forgot to eat lunch or dinner. But then I married Sherie, and I had to change my schedule to make time for her. Some years later, children came along and my schedule changed even more so that I would have time for our kids, too. Typically, a lot of major changes occur between the ages of twenty and thirty. Life as a single, young minister is different from life for a married, young minister. Also, a couple with one child has a different life than a couple with three or four kids, all under the age of seven.

The seasons of life must be considered when setting our schedule. Key questions should be addressed.

- When a couple has infants or young children, are the husband and wife encouraged to spend sufficient time with their children?

- Are they expected to attend just as many meetings as an associate who has grown children?

These are sensitive topics, particularly in multi-staff churches. I'm not saying that ministers who are single have all the time in the world and therefore should attend every church or ministry meeting. How this balance works out should be customized at each church or ministry but the "seasons of life" must be considered.

As I said earlier, it is best to ask these questions before taking a ministry position. But what often happens is that a single, young minister interviews for a position thinking only of himself and his schedule as a single guy. And then, a few months or years later, he gets married. Then, two years later or so their first child arrives. The minister's expectations toward his life and ministry have changed. Now he needs time to spend with his wife and infant.

Or, a couple will interview for a position at a church, thinking of their schedule as a couple without children. Then, two years into the marriage, they decide to have kids, and they find that their schedule is out of whack.

Though I recommend that young ministers understand their boss's expectations before taking a job, I understand that while they're in their twenties many changes will occur. Adapting to these changes will require "negotiations" with your boss. I've found that the overwhelming majority of bosses understand the seasons of life and how that affects a young minister's priorities.

Generational Differences

There are generational issues in this discussion. As one older minister stated, "The mindset of the younger crowd is different from that of the older crowd. The younger crowd struggles with sacrificing your family for God."

In one interview a minister, about age fifty-five, said it this way:

> The older generation, my generation, said that their priorities were God, family, and then ministry. But a lot of us didn't really follow those priorities. Instead, it was God, ministry, and then family. In contrast, the younger generation seems intent on keeping the order of God, family, and then ministry.

I heard this opinion from several older ministers. They acknowledged that their generation said that their priorities should be in the order of

God, family, and then ministry, but that in truth and action, it was God, ministry, and then family.

It would be easy to resort to "older minister bashing," but the truth is that any generation can easily slip into misplaced priorities. The main lesson is for every generation to shoot toward the goal of healthy life and ministry priorities.

Evaluate Your Pace

In high school I was on the track team and I had a teammate, Lee, who was about 6'3" and weighed 240 lbs. Lee was a good friend and our team's shot putter. At one track meet our 400-meter runner did not show up and the coach asked if someone would volunteer to substitute for him. Lee volunteered and for some reason the coach let him run the race. But Lee had never run the 400-meter race, a quarter mile, which is one lap around most tracks. In the 400-meter race it is wise to pace yourself at the beginning of the race so you have some energy left to sprint the final 100 meters. But contrary to a wise running strategy, once the starting gun sounded Lee broke into an all-out sprint while the other runners were pacing themselves.

At the first turn Lee was in first place and even as they reached the halfway point he was still in first. But then, noticeably, he lost energy and gradually slowed down until all the other runners had passed him and, as Lee was "running" the final 100 meters, the other runners were way ahead of him. All of us teammates were cheering him on during the entire race, but as he headed down the home stretch we cheered him on, not to win, but just hoping he would finish. At that point he was far behind all the other runners and just a few yards before the finish line he had exhausted all his energy and collapsed in a heap on the cinder track. Fortunately, other than a few cuts and scrapes from the cinders, once he caught his breath he was fine. We ran to him, pulled him onto the grass infield, and congratulated him on giving it all and almost finishing.

It is wise to ask, "If you maintain your present pace, what will be the result for you and your marriage and family?" Life and ministry are not sprints; they are 400-meter events, or even marathons. There are seasons in ministry when we must work extra long hours but we should determine that normally we will work at a pace that is sustainable and that won't harm the family/work balance.

One older minister reflected on what he has seen among the younger crowd: "Too often, youth pastors are trying to keep up with an older person who is in a different season of life." The lesson? Keep your expectations realistic.

Earlier I mentioned a senior pastor who required his staff members to spend four nights per week with their families. Why did he have this requirement? I can only guess because I've never talked with him, but perhaps he believes that for his staff members to stay with him at the church for the long haul, they would need to find the proper balance between ministry and family.

Here is how a young minister described how he and his wife experienced this challenge:

> When my wife and I were married we worked long and hard at the church. We did plenty of "extra" work. Then we had our first child. That kind of forced the issue. It caused us to ask questions. I decided that I would be more valuable if I endured, if I work longer. If I had continued in the pace I had kept, I knew I would not last long as a minister or youth pastor. Now I take a day Mondays off. Lately I've been doing better—we, as a family, get in the car and go somewhere together.

That is a good model to follow.

Cultural Issues

In some cultures this need for balance is even more pronounced than in other cultures. For example, I have friends who minister in Hispanic churches and they say that in the Hispanic culture all staff and their spouses are expected to show up almost every time the church doors are open. Likewise, a Korean friend informed me that in Korea the preferred priority order is as follows: God, ministry, and then family. They believe that is the correct order for priorities.

What are we to do with these differences? Do I proclaim that my way is biblical and that other cultures are sinning? I think not. Though I think that it's important to find the correct balance, and that means not neglecting family, I recognize that the expectations of your spouse and children play a major role in this issue. Their expectations are a key to understanding this issue. Earlier I stated that in families and marriage, love is spelled "time." That is true but just how much time that involves is up to the specific family and spouse.

Paul addressed this subject when writing about whether to marry or remain single:

> In everything you do, I want you to be free from the concerns of this life. An unmarried man can spend his time doing the Lord's work and thinking how to please him. But a married man can't do that so well. He has to think about his earthly responsibilities and how to please his wife. His interests are divided. In the same way, a woman who is no longer married or has never been married can be more devoted to the Lord in body and in spirit, while the married woman must be concerned about her earthly responsibilities and how to please her husband. (1 Cor. 7:32-34, NLT)

Paul writes that a husband "*has to think about* his earthly responsibilities and how to please his wife." And a wife "*must be concerned about* her earthly responsibilities and how to please her husband." There is no debate whether this is the right thing to do. It's simply accepted as the correct thing to do. But the determination of how much time to spend together may differ from family to family.

Ministers can be so driven to work for the Lord that they easily slip into neglect of their families. God calls us to love others, and that begins with our own families.

Questions for Young Leaders

1. What are the forces in your life that could throw off the balance between work and family?

2. How have the seasons of life affected your ability to maintain a balance between work and family?

3. Have you and your spouse discussed this issue of work/family balance? If so, what are the main concerns of your spouse?

Questions for Lead Pastors or Ministry Directors

1. In this chapter I state that the younger generation of ministers views the work/family balance differently than older generations. Do you agree? If so, how has this difference in perspective been reflected in your work situations or the situations of your friends and colleagues?

2. How can you help the young ministers who work with you develop a healthy work/family balance?

3. What are the expectations of the official board of your church or ministry toward you and your staff in regard to this issue of work/family balance?

Recommendations for Lead Pastors or Ministry Directors

1. In staff meetings emphasize the need for all leadership team members to maintain a work/family balance, and the need to periodically make adjustments that lead toward this balance.

2. Set parameters for team leaders regarding how many nights a week they can spend at the church or office doing ministry work. For example, one pastor requires that every married leadership team member must spend four nights a week at home with family.

Challenge # 10

Conversations and Adjustments
Leading Toward Balance

The purpose of this chapter is to provide direction that will help you work with your spouse to find the correct balance in your work and marriage/family priorities.

Too often, young ministers don't talk to their spouses about balance between work and family. Perhaps they sense the dissatisfaction in their spouse and are afraid that talking about it will only result in a disagreement or a logjam. But it's wise to talk about it.

In the pages that follow I cite three issues that the husband and wife should discuss. I will refer to the husband as the one who is the primary leader in full-time ministry because that is the most common situation.

Issue #1 – Determine the Level of Satisfaction or Frustration

The first issue is to determine if there is satisfaction with the present balance between work and family. If there is frustration due to imbalance then determine the level or intensity of that frustration.

One young minister stated,

> Several times my wife has said, "Why are we doing ministry? My life is sucked into your life. The salary is low. You have a day off and we plan to do something

together as a family, but then you are asked to do a funeral. I ask if you can do something about it but you can't, you have to do the funeral."

You can hear the frustration in her words.

In discussing the matter with his wife a young minister first needs to determine her level of frustration. Recognize that everyone experiences some frustration in balancing work and personal life; ministers are not the only ones to find it challenging. But it's important to determine the level of frustration. If the wife is ready to walk away from the marriage and family due to her high level of frustration, that is different than the normal kinds of frustration everyone faces at times. Both kinds of frustration should be addressed but one calls for triage, emergency-room kind of attention, the other for candid discussion.

It's easy for young ministers to ignore this issue, hoping it will just go away or that it really doesn't exist. But it is better to recognize it, discuss it, and find ways to deal with it.

Issue #2 – Wives: How Important is Your Husband's Call to Ministry?

A second issue to consider is the level of the wife's "call" to ministry, or the level of the wife's commitment to her husband and his ministry. (Once again, in this discussion I'm primarily addressing the husband who is a minister.)

One thirty-five-year old minister commented:

> I have a friend who quit the ministry because his wife simply said, "No more." Even in my own life, one time my wife said to me, "Can't you just do some other line of work?" A wife must ask herself, "Your husband's call to ministry—where does that stand in your list of priorities?" That is an important question.

Some time ago, I formulated four models of ministry and marriage that I have seen among pastors in the local church. The models are cited below:

Four Models of Ministry and Marriage in Pastoral Ministry:

Model #1:
Both husband and wife feel called to ministry. They are in competition.
Result: Not healthy, due to the competition.

Model #2:
Both husband and wife feel called to ministry. They don't have a competitive relationship but are working well together in ministry.
Result: Healthy.

Model #3:
The husband feels called to ministry but the wife doesn't feel a formal "call" to ministry. However, she is very committed to her work in the church and loves her involvement in the church.
Result: Healthy. The wife doesn't need to have a distinct call to ministry. She is involved and committed.

Model #4:
The husband feels called to ministry but the wife doesn't have a call to ministry. The wife puts up with her husband's ministry but she doesn't enjoy involvement in the church. She leads a separate life from her husband's ministry and the church.
Result: Not healthy.

I cited these four models when interviewing pastors, and asked for their response. A number of them said they'd seen model number four among colleagues during their years in ministry and that it isn't a pleasant situation for the couple.

One forty-five-year-old minister said the following: "If the wife is just putting up with the ministry aspect of 'the ministry,' that is trouble, especially in the young years. That is miserable. A husband who is a lead pastor with a wife like that is 'stuck' for the rest of his life." I would add that most likely the wife, too, feels stuck.

Issue #3 - Ministry Will Suck Up
the Minister's Wife's Time

There exists a certain inequality in the ministry when the husband is in pastoral ministry but the wife is working a secular job. A man who is pastoring will find that church activities tend to almost demand that both he and his wife are involved in the church or ministry, but the minister will usually not find the same level of demand from his wife's secular work.

A young minister summed it up by saying, "The ministry demands for my wife are enormous. Ministry has the tendency to 'suck up' not only the minister's time, but also the minister's wife's time. In contrast, if the wife works, her work will usually not suck up the time of her minister-husband."

The solution to this problem is that the young minister must realize that his wife has a life, too. She has a "calendar." Respect must be given to the wife's time, too.

Conclusion: I've cited three specific issues. There may be other issues that the husband and wife should discuss when considering this issue of ministry and family balance. The important key is to actually take the time to discuss these issues and come to a resolution. These are not issues that you can discuss once and never discuss again. They are issues that should be revisited from time to time.

Working with Your Leader to Find the Correct Balance

You should be aware that there is variety among leaders (bosses) regarding this issue of balancing family and work. Most leaders recognize the need for this balance and they practice and preach a healthy balance. In fact, some leaders are more protective of their associates' family/work balance than are the associates, in part because they have seen over the years how that imbalance can destroy a family. However, there are some, hopefully few, leaders who are willing to sacrifice their families in order to succeed in their ministry. For example, they may believe that all ministers should be working seven days a week, with no time off.

Whatever your leader's perspective on this issue of family/work balance, your first step in addressing it is to be aware of that perspective.

Don't assume you know others' perspectives, particularly when applying for a ministry position. When you are interviewing for a youth pastor or associate position, thoughtfully ask about the pastor's policy regarding days off, spouse involvement, etc. (spell out the specific issues). Consider those policies seriously before making a ministry position decision.

Remember that actions speak louder than words. If your lead pastor isn't modeling a healthy balance, as his associate you will have a tough time finding balance.

Leaders don't always comprehend the needs facing young ministers' marriages and families, and neither do young ministers always understand the pressures facing the senior leaders. More two-way communication is needed. Two key questions are:

+ Do leaders listen to their associates' concerns regarding balance between family and ministry?
+ Do associates understand the pressures that the leader is facing?

Communicate Your Priorities to Others

If you are a youth pastor or associate pastor, don't expect everyone in your church to understand that you and your family need time together. They may have unrealistic expectations toward you in this regard and therefore place unneeded pressure on you and your family. For example, though you may have your boss's permission to miss some church events, some church people may look for you at church functions and not understand why you are not present. You may need to spend some time and effort educating them on the need for balance in family and work.

Mid-Course Adjustments

To have a successful ministry and marriage, couples must be willing to make adjustments in both the marriage and the ministry. I refer to these as the M & M adjustments, short for Marriage & Ministry adjustments. M & M adjustments are those times in a married couple's life when they must work out solutions that involve finding the proper balance between their marriage and their ministry. You can't ignore the problem. Discussions must be intentional. Marriages and ministries have ended because the husband was not aware of the problem or because the couple did not take the time to deal with the problem. To thrive in their marriages and ministries, ministers must make adjustments in their families and ministries. Planning our ministry before we start is important, but just as important is making adjustments as we journey together. Priorities and circumstances change along the way and we must make the proper adjustments.

Making adjustments in our marriage and ministry is not unlike driving from Los Angeles to Chicago. As I plan such a trip I have a choice between a southern route through Arizona, New Mexico and Oklahoma and then northwest to Chicago, or I can choose a more northerly route by driving across Nevada, Utah, Nebraska, and Iowa, then straight west to Chicago. I make my driving plans in advance, but I also know that bad weather and highway construction may cause me to alter my route. I make adjustments along the way.

Taking a long trip has some parallels to marriage and ministry. As a young married minister I had some fixed ideas regarding how Sherie and I needed to work out our lives and ministries. But once we were involved in the ministry together we had to continually consider the adjustments in our marriage and ministry.

Adjustments in Schedule and Priorities

One adjustment that must be worked out is in regard to schedules and priorities.

One minister related his experience early in his marriage.

> In the early years of our marriage, we were going different directions. I felt that my wife would be part of my ministry, and she felt that I would be part of her ministry. I was the youth pastor and felt part of that [young] crowd, of course. So after church on Sunday night I would want her to come and be with me and the young people. But she was in the music ministry and after church she wanted to go out to eat with the music

crowd. So we were heading in different directions and it was causing some friction.

This pastor then described how he and his wife finally reached a point where they had to sit down and talk about it. They finally worked out a solution that worked for both of them. They made adjustments along the way.

Adjustments in Boundaries

Another area that must be adjusted is in regard to the boundaries that ministers and their spouses must set.

One minister's wife had been struggling with a bad attitude toward her husband when she started attending a women's meeting at the church. She found that before, during, and after the meeting many of these ladies would criticize their husbands. The minister's wife decided that she needed to set a boundary. She felt that if she continued meeting with these ladies she would only feed her bad attitude toward her husband. However, she knew that if she quit the women's group it would hurt her ministry. She was in a bind. She resolved it by setting a boundary. She told her husband that she was making a promise to him that from that moment on she would never criticize him publicly. It was a boundary she readily set in order to preserve their marriage intimacy. Over the years she has kept to that promise. When in private, they talk openly, but in public, she never criticizes him. (It would have been interesting to learn if her lack of criticism compelled other ladies in that group to stop their criticizing.)

Boundaries are individualized. Only you understand the areas of your life and ministry where you must set the boundaries to preserve or build your individual or married lives. Ask yourself the following questions:

- Where am I failing in my life or in my marriage?
- Or, if you are single, you can ask where you are failing in your relationships with others.

Often the failures can be traced to inadequate, or a lack of, boundaries that we have set. What boundaries do you need to set to preserve or build your life?

Adjustments Regarding Expectations

Another ministry and marriage adjustment for married couples is in regard to expectations toward the spouse. The wife may see significant faults or weaknesses in the life or ministry of her husband. Maybe she believes that his teaching and preaching lack enthusiasm, or perhaps she observes that he waits too long to make important ministry decisions. Conversely, maybe the husband finds some things lacking with his wife. Maybe his wife has a tough time relating to the girls in the youth group, or perhaps she has a tough time finding her ministry niche in the church. We must be aware of our expectations. Then we must intentionally decide if and how to address them before they affect our relationship and ministry. Ask yourself the following:

+ What are my husband's/wife's strengths?
+ What are my husband's/wife's faults and weaknesses?
+ And then the key question: What should I do about those faults and weaknesses?

My recommendation is threefold:

First, don't try to change your spouse. Your emphasis should be on loving your spouse in spite of his or her weaknesses and faults. Learn to gladly love and live with your spouse as he or she is. When you pray, instead of constantly asking God to change your spouse, ask God to change you to make you more forgiving and kind.

Second, be your spouse's biggest cheerleader. Be an encourager. When your spouse does something good, tell him or her.

Third, learn how to speak the truth in love. Learn if and when it is appropriate to talk to your spouse about his or her weaknesses. Candid feedback is appreciated when it is offered in the right context and at the right time.

Consider what one young husband had to say:

> My wife is a real encourager. When things are tough and we talk, she encourages me to "hang in there and be faithful." She is supportive. Sometimes she tells me, "You are a great youth pastor." At other times, she tells me the negative. I made a bad decision at camp one time as to what time we would depart from the camp and

head home. Everyone else had vacated the camp by noon, and I had told our youth group that we would leave at 1 PM. She said, "What were you thinking? Everyone always leaves by noon." So, she tells me the truth, too. Sometimes it is a reality check.

This couple was learning how to deal with each others' expectations.

I have observed over the years that a minister who grew up in a minister's home may expect his wife to act like his mom. He may expect his wife to "do" ministry like his mom did ministry. On the other hand, a pastor's daughter who is now a pastor's wife may expect her husband to "do" ministry like her father did it. But often these expectations are unrealistic. Everybody is unique.

I was watching Franklin Graham on TV recently and I wondered how many times people have assumed that Franklin should be just like his dad, Billy Graham; they expect Franklin to preach and travel just like his dad has done. Their assumptions could easily be strengthened by the fact that Franklin looks and talks a lot like his dad. Fortunately, Franklin has found his own niche in the body of Christ.

For those who grew up in a minister's home, remember that your husband is not your dad! Your wife is not your mother! For some of you, that is delightful news. For others, you may not have thought about these expectations. When we expect others to act like another person or do ministry like a parent did it, we place that person in a ministry straightjacket. That can be suffocating. We must recognize the expectations we bring to our ministry marriages and then free our husbands and wives to be who they are. Yes, they will naturally carry some of their parents' skills and attitudes into the ministry and marriage. But in other ways they will be very different, and that is the uniqueness that God has created within them. Be thankful for who they are!

Husbands, especially, must be patient with their wives as the wives learn to find their niche in the church. One minister related that it took it took two years for his wife to "find" a "call" to the ministry. With her, the "call" came through a lengthy string of experiences. She reflected, "At first I felt like I was just tagging along on his ministry and that I didn't really have my own ministry niche." Fortunately, during a weekend retreat that was full of quiet devotional times, she "found" her call. Following the retreat she felt like a full partner in the ministry. It all clicked.

Trust is obviously a big issue in marriage. Wives may need to come to a point where they cross over into a new threshold of trust in their husbands who are ministers. At one point one wife told her husband, "I realize that I have to honor you as the head of our house and ministry. Whatever God calls you to do, I'll assume you are on your knees. Let's let God handle it."

Every husband and wife team is unique. You react to the ministry in your own way and face unique challenges. The point is that you must make adjustments as you go along in ministry. If you aren't aware of the fact that you must make adjustments, and if you then neglect making them, you may jeopardize your ministries and perhaps your marriage.

The Priority

In some situations, you may feel that you have no alternative but to choose between work and family. Perhaps you've tried and tried to work out the differences with your boss but it hasn't worked. Perhaps incessant pressure from a powerful person in the church makes you feel as though you've been backed into a corner. If you feel forced to make a choice between your work and your family, choose your family and marriage. God will honor your choice. But normally it will not come to that. Once you discuss your challenges with others you can usually work it out.

Questions for Young Leaders

1. What adjustments have you made in your marriage and/or ministry in order to maintain a healthy balance?

2. I cited four marriage and ministry models in this chapter. Which model describes your situation?

3. Have you discussed the marriage/ministry balance with your lead pastor or director? If so, what conclusions did you reach?

4. I titled one subsection, "Ministry Will Suck up the Minister's Wife's Time." Have you seen that this is true? How should a young couple handle this issue?

5. What boundaries have you and your spouse set in order to develop and maintain a healthy marriage and ministry balance?

Questions for Lead Pastors or Ministry Directors

1. Think about the young leaders working with you. Which of them have developed a healthy balance between marriage and ministry? Which of them are struggling with this issue?

2. What can you do to help your young leaders struggling with this issue?

3. I cited four marriage and ministry models in this chapter. Looking back on your years of ministry, can you think of friends who fit each model? If so, what were the implications of their choices?

Recommendations for Lead Pastors or Ministry Directors

1. Be a sounding board, or even a counselor, for young ministers who are making these marriage and ministry adjustments.

2. Lead a discussion on this issue in a staff meeting.

3. Ask your young leaders how the policies and culture of the church or ministry encourage or discourage a healthy balance between marriage and ministry.

Work Relationship Challenges

Challenge # 11
―――――
Understanding Your Boss

I use the term "boss" in this chapter though I know that in most churches associates don't refer to the lead pastor as "the boss." However, this book is directed to a variety of Christian leaders in a wide variety of ministry positions so I've chosen to use this term here.

When we nourish our relationship with our boss, and when they do the same with us, there is a payoff. It is cited in Psalm 133 (NLT).

> How wonderful it is, how pleasant,
> when brothers live together in harmony!
> For harmony is as precious as the fragrant anointing oil
> that was poured over Aaron's head,
> that ran down his beard
> and onto the border of his robe.
> Harmony is as refreshing as the dew from Mount Hermon
> that falls on the mountains of Zion.
> And the Lord has pronounced his blessing,
> even life forevermore.

At least two results are mentioned here for those who find harmony with their leader, their boss: The first positive result is a pleasant atmosphere. The second is the blessing of the Lord.

I have friends who started out in ministry with me and are no longer in ministry. Many left the ministry due to problems that started with their relationship with their boss. They just couldn't, or didn't, get along with the boss.

One minister spoke of the significance of an associate's relationship to his lead pastor.

> Personally, as I reflect on my first three years as an associate I conclude that it is so important who you work for. Choosing wisely who you work for is more important than the church you work at. The young minister should be able to say, "I'd like to be like him [the lead pastor], rather than using the salary or the church as the deciding factor."

The relationship you have with your boss is important! This is the case not only among Christian leaders, but also among a variety of other leaders. Vecchio, in his book, *Leaders*, writes to a broad audience. He says, "The number one reason people leave their jobs is a bad relationship with their boss."[30]

Making a case for nourishing your relationship with your boss, Vecchio continues: "Recent studies suggest that effective managers take time and effort to manage not only relationships with their subordinates but also those with their bosses."[31]

That quote is so subtle that it's easy to miss his point. Vecchio is saying that we put a lot of emphasis on handling our relationships with those who work under us but not enough on those who are over us.

Vecchio continues by highlighting a common mistake: "Some managers who *actively* and effectively supervise subordinates, products, markets, and technologies assume an almost *passively* reactive stance vis-à-vis their bosses. Such a stance almost always hurts them and their companies." (Italics added)[32]

We should actively concentrate on developing our relationship with our boss.

If we sat and talked with youth pastors who were just beginning their ministry and we asked them to tell us their priorities for the first years in ministry, we would hear about many worthy priorities. We would hear about the need to actively evangelize teenagers, build a good relationship with the parents, and maintain their own fervor for the Lord. All of those are important. But my guess is that few would mention the necessity of working hard to build a positive relationship with their boss, the lead pastor. As Vecchio points out, we too often take a passive stance with that relationship. We assume that the youth pastor/lead pastor relationship will sort of take care of itself. But often it doesn't. And the result is what was stated above: "The number one reason people leave their jobs is a bad relationship with their boss."

I have been coaching leaders nearly full time now for nine years. I've found plenty of evidence to back up this point: Some of a Christian leader's greatest challenges will be found in his relationship with his boss.

Most likely at some point in these pages you will ask, "You seem to be saying that I need to do everything to nourish my relationship with my boss. But what about him? Doesn't he have a responsibility to me, too?" Yes, your boss should take all these issues to heart, too, and seek to understand how best to relate to you, his associate. But you can't change your boss. However, you can change how you approach your relationship with him. My purpose in this book is to focus on the young minister.

I think that the "top-down" leadership approach doesn't work like it did in the past. Young and older leaders alike seem more attracted today to the idea of teamwork and more egalitarian leadership and are less impressed with authoritarian leadership. But I don't know if your boss has bought into this change in approach. If you understand the concepts in this chapter and apply them to your relationship with your boss you will help that relationship move along. Hopefully your boss will reciprocate and meet you halfway, but my experience tells me that some will not and that much of the responsibility may fall on you.

I interviewed a lead pastor recently who has guys lining up (symbolically) to work on his staff because they've heard from their friends that he considers his pastoral staff members, even the young ones, as integral members of their church leadership team. That lead pastor does not practice a top-down approach but focuses on building a team where each associate has input and respect. It's no wonder that this lead pastor has guys lining up to work with him. Hopefully, if you are on staff at a church, you're working with a lead pastor like that.

If you don't work with that kind of boss you can do some things to improve your relationship with him or her. It starts with a question: Are you nourishing your relationship with your boss? In the next pages I cite several ideas that will help you increase your understanding of your boss, and hopefully improve your relationship.

Know Your Leader

You will help yourself if you seek to understand everything you can about your boss. This understanding will provide clues regarding the degree of "fit" between you and your boss, ways to work well together, and possible conflicts with him or her.

There will be things in your relationship with your boss that you want to change. Perhaps you want him to take more time to mentor you, or perhaps you want more face-to-face meetings with your boss. You will be more persuasive in your discussions with him if you seek to understand him or her first.

In particular, there are four general areas of life and ministry that you would do well to understand. They are your boss's...

1. values
2. preferred work culture
3. pressures
4. strengths, weaknesses, and blind spots

Your Boss's Values

What are your boss's values? A Christian leader's values are the key or top-priority principles describing who he intends to be, and determining how he intends to do church or his ministry. They identify a leader's core philosophy that drives how he does ministry, determines his priorities, and informs his decisions.[33]

Sometimes your leader will clearly articulate his values. Consider what this fifty-seven-year-old former lead pastor had to say about young leaders:

> When I was a young youth pastor, I worked for guys whose goal was not creativity, but productivity. They were concerned with numbers. Then I became a lead

pastor. I really enjoyed having the young staff members. Their greatest challenge was that creativity was their goal. My frustration was that the young ministers focused too much on creativity and not enough on productivity. I really enjoyed their creativity, but the problem was that after creating they were ready to go home. I was more concerned with productivity. Are we seeing numbers increase? Are there more here this week than last week? That was one of my biggest challenges.

Do you see the values of this leader? Specifically, he contrasts creativity and productivity. He sees them as two separate values, although they are not inherently in opposition. Most leaders would consider both as important, but this leader definitely sees productivity as of greater value than creativity. Smart young leaders understand the values of their boss and how those values align with or differ from his own values.

To identify your leader's values, ask the following questions:

Question #1:

What distinguishes your leader's ministry from other leaders? Is it an emphasis on evangelism, feeding the poor, foreign missions, community involvement, or is it all the above? Most likely, when you interviewed for your present ministry position, your leader's values were articulated, at least to some degree. Try to identify them.

Question #2:

Why are people attracted to your church? What do people say about your ministry?

If you are in a local church, what is it that people say pulled them toward your church? Was it the lively worship, the emphasis on small groups, excellent teaching? The answers to those questions will provide the key to understanding your leader's values, particularly if your lead pastor has been at the church for some time and has had time to shape the ministries and programs of your church.

Question #3:

What does your leader get passionate about? What makes him happy, and what makes him angry?

Note your leader's personal responses to life's circumstances. His responses will demonstrate his values.

For example, we understand one of the apostle Paul's values from his experiences with John Mark. Remember that John Mark had deserted Paul and his team early in their missionary journeys. Later when John Mark wanted to accompany them on another missionary trip Paul was opposed to the idea. Paul was so passionate about this issue that he and Barnabas parted ways over it. I would define Paul's value as follows: Workers on his team must be willing to endure hardship in ministry.

Now that you have thought through these questions, what would you list as your boss's top five values?

Your Boss's Top Five Values

_____
_____
_____
_____
_____

Follow this with an identification of your values. (You may need to review the three questions above to identify your own.)

Your Top Five Values

_____
_____
_____
_____
_____

Now, compare your values and your boss's values. How similar are your values and your boss's values?

What conclusions can you draw from this comparison?

Your Boss's Preferred Work Culture

Related to the leader's leadership values is his preferred ministry culture. Your boss most definitely has a certain ministry culture that he is comfortable with. Often the elements of this culture are subconscious.

Sometimes you discover them when he says, "That's just not the way we do things around here."

What kind of ministry culture is your boss fostering in your ministry? Consider the differences between the following two missionary organizations.

A comparison of the characteristics of two missionary organizations:

Organization 1	*Organization 2*
paper culture	oral culture
policy driven	idea driven
reserved	cutting edge
historically driven	future driven
traditional	avant-garde
little change	constant change
coats and ties	jeans and t-shirts
quiet	noisy
low tech	high tech
slow pace	kinetic pace[34]

I heard of a ministry office where the boss would not allow coffee cups because he wanted to minimize the informal atmosphere. He preferred a formal work atmosphere. That is certainly not my kind of work place but each leader has particular preferences.

One youth pastor told us of a lead pastor who didn't call a staff meeting for the five years the youth pastor worked for him. That is unhealthy for any ministry but I mention it to say that each leader is different and an assistant will only help himself and the ministry if he understands the leader's idiosyncrasies.

Your Boss's Preferred and Actual Work Culture

Think about the culture of the church or ministry where you and your boss work. Which of these two cultures cited above best describes your boss's preferred work culture, the culture he prefers most? Next, ask this question: Which of the words above (in either list) would you use to describe your church or ministry's actual culture? Then, follow up that question with two more: Is there a good fit between your boss's preferred work culture and your ministry's current culture? Does your answer shed any light on the joys and frustrations that you and your leader experience in your ministry?

Your Preferred Work Culture

Now think about yourself and your preferences. Which of the two cultures do you prefer? Most young ministers today probably prefer culture #2. An awareness of the congruence between your boss's culture and your preferred work culture provides a deeper understanding of the joys and frustrations you experience as you work with your boss.

Other Relevant Questions:

+ Does your boss prefer informal interactions with assistants, or a more businesslike and formal style?
+ Does your boss like to get information through memos, formal meetings, or phone calls?
+ Does your boss thrive on conflict or try to minimize it?

Pressures

Your boss is answerable to another person or a board. Do you understand the pressures inherent in his position? Pressures on leaders normally involve metrics such as finances and numbers. In a church those metrics are normally church offerings and worship service attendance. Too often we're aware of our own personal and work pressures but not especially aware of the pressures facing our bosses.

Following are key questions to consider:

+ What pressures does your boss face from the official board of your church or ministry?
+ What pressures does your boss face from key people in the church or ministry?
+ What pressures does your boss face from other stakeholders, such as civic leaders, denominational leaders, or special interest groups?
+ How is your perspective of the ministry or church different from your boss's perspective?

You might sit down with your boss over lunch and ask him about his philosophy related to those two metrics of ministry finances and numbers (attendance, enrollment, etc.). You could ask, "What are the keys to financial soundness in our ministry?" Or you might ask, "How should we as a staff think about the significance of numbers in our ministry or church?" Every leader has a philosophy, though it is not always explicit. The book of Proverbs states that a wise man draws out the thoughts of the king. Similarly, through your questions you can better understand the leader you work with.

Don't forget to consider the pressures a minister receives from his or her spouse and family. In fact, a wise young minister will also concentrate on developing a positive relationship with the boss's spouse.

Strengths, Weaknesses, & Blind Spots

Learn all you can about your leader's strong and weak points. Blind spots are simply weaknesses that the leader is unaware of. Someone once told me that you can view leaders through three lenses: How does your leader do in …

1. communication
2. administration
3. care and concern

Communication involves both interpersonal communication and public speaking.

Administration has to do with how he or she handles meetings, people, and finances.

Care and concern have to do with how he comes across: Is he seen as caring, involved, and warm? Or, is he detached and cold?

Who Adjusts?

Every boss has a work style that he prefers. The ideal is that both the boss and the staff member are aware of their own styles and adjust them to each other. The ideal is that there is a give and take, that there is teamwork. But this book is written primarily for the young leader so I have addressed this challenge from the perspective of the young leader.

Research has shown that some staff members derail because they are unable or unwilling to adapt to bosses with leadership styles different from their own. I wish that I could tell you that your boss will meet you halfway, and that he will take your styles into consideration, but that may not happen. However, you can enhance your relationship with your boss by understanding his preferred work style and culture, and making adjustments to his style.

Questions for Young Leaders

1. How is your relationship with your boss? What words would you use to describe it?

2. What could you do to improve your relationship with your boss?

3. I asked you to understand your boss's values, preferred work culture, pressures, and strengths, weaknesses, and blind spots. As you've reflected on these aspects of your boss's life, what lessons or thoughts have stood out?

4. What aspects of your workplace culture do you like the most? What aspects do you dislike?

Questions for Lead Pastors or Ministry Directors

1. I quoted an author who said, "The number-one reason people leave their jobs is a bad relationship with their boss." What do you think are the top three reasons for the poor relationship that people have with their bosses?

2. What are the positive and negative points of the present-day emphasis upon team leadership in the church and in ministries?

3. How is your relationship with each of the young leaders you work with? How could you improve each relationship?

4. What would you like each of your young leaders to understand about you and your work style?

Recommendations for Lead Pastors or Ministry Directors

1. Take some time to write out your values, preferred work culture, pressures, and strengths & weaknesses.

2. Consider how your values, culture, etc. compare with those of the young leaders who work with you.

Challenge # 12

Your Boss: Imperfections, Triangulation, and Candid Dialogue

How should we respond when we see faults in our boss? And what if we disagree with our boss on specific issues; how should we handle that? In this chapter we move from simply understanding our boss to dealing with some of the challenges that arise in the midst of this important relationship.

Imperfect Bosses

During the summer between my sophomore and junior year in college I worked for three months at a men's Christian rehabilitation center in Texas. I didn't interview for this short-term position—it was an arranged practicum for which I would earn six semester credits from my college (if I wrote an acceptable paper describing my experiences).

I had some very positive experiences that summer. But I also had some negative experiences, mostly of my own making. The greatest challenge I had was respecting my boss. I noticed all kinds of faults in him. He was too authoritarian. He was disorganized. He wasn't spiritual enough. He did a lot of things poorly, at least in my estimation. (I imagine he had a few opinions regarding my faults, too). I had a lousy attitude toward him. Due to my negative viewpoint I had difficulty submitting to his leadership.

One day the Lord spoke to my heart about my attitude. In order for you to understand God's word to me that day I need to mention that every day from about two to five PM all of us worked in the ministry's large garden that provided food for the rehab center. Do you know that in August it is blazing hot in southern Texas? Every day we worked in back-breaking conditions as laborers in the hot, Texas sun. One day as we worked I was inwardly complaining to God about the leadership faults of my boss. I was thirsty and tired and sweating. I was miserable. And the Lord spoke these words to me in my spirit: "The rebellious live in a sun-scorched land." It was like the Lord pierced my heart with a spear. I realized that He was rebuking me for my attitude toward my boss, telling me that just as my skin was sun-scorched due to the hot Texas sun, my spirit was sun-scorched because of my rebellious attitude toward my boss. Only later did I realize that the sentence, "The rebellious live in a sun-scorched land," was actually from Psalm 68:6 (NIV).

That day I changed my attitude. From then on I listened and obeyed my boss with a positive attitude. I changed my thinking, too, so that while working in the hot sun I consciously thanked God for my work and for my boss. After that, though I worked strenuously in a sun-scorched land my inner person experienced a refreshing peace. I learned a valuable lesson that summer.

Everybody knows that all bosses have faults. It is one thing to know that. It is another to experience those faults on a weekly basis. (Of course, every assistant has faults, too). Let's take a moment and cite some of the most common faults that young ministers see in their bosses. The following descriptions are from my interviews with young ministers.

One complaint is that the boss rarely communicates with the young leader and when he does communicate it is to discuss the young leader's missteps. For example, youth pastors want to informally discuss various aspects of the ministry but find that the lead pastor is rarely available for such discussions. Another common complaint is that the boss is disorganized. The disorganization causes a general lack of efficiency in the ministry and reflects negatively on the entire staff. Another one is that the boss is insecure. The young leader feels that he is viewed with suspicion by the boss. A further complaint is that the boss is too demanding of the young leader, particularly in regard to the results the boss expects in the young leader's ministry. It may relate to the amount of extra time that the leader expects the young leader and his family to devote to church activities. Another complaint is that the boss doesn't take responsibility for his own mistakes. Young leaders recount stories where their boss inferred to the congregation that the blame for a mistake should be laid at the feet of staff members when it was actually the boss's fault.

Those were the common complaints that emerged through interviews with young leaders. I imagine that bosses who are reading this feel like they are being attacked or unjustly singled out. That is not my purpose here. My purpose is to state the common complaints of young ministers and then suggest healthy responses for young leaders.

Healthy Responses

Let's consider a number of healthy responses to the faults of those we work with.

One solution is to interview wisely for ministry positions. This is an odd solution because it is a "solution-before-the-problem-exists." When you interview for a position, ask specific questions of your boss so that you aren't caught unaware after taking the position.

For example, let's consider the first fault cited above, that the boss talks to the young minister only when there is a problem. What if, during the interview process, you asked the lead pastor how often he expects to meet with you individually if you are hired. If you're interested in being mentored by your boss you might mention that interest in the interview and see if your boss is willing to take on that role.

Second, it's important to watch your attitude. You'll never have a perfect boss (and you'll never be a perfect boss). Remember that David respected King Saul even though Saul didn't deserve it. Live your life giving grace—unmerited favor—to others.

Check your attitude. An interesting thing about attitudes is that they are caught—you don't need to say a thing to others but they will "catch" your attitude. You have a choice: You can influence others (who are watching you) toward grace or toward bitterness. Don't stir up bitterness. Stir up grace and mercy!

Third, show proper respect to your boss, particularly in public settings. In public if you speak about your boss at all, always do so with respect, speaking proudly of the positive and not mentioning the negative.

While talking with people at the church potluck insert a compliment into your conversation regarding your lead pastor.

I've met young leaders who, in spite of repeated attempts, just can't seem to work well with their bosses. I advised them to consider leaving and finding a new position. If you can't respect your leader then it may be time to move on to another position. Don't waste your life. And don't infect the others in that ministry. There are plenty of other leaders out there who are fully deserving of your respect.

A final key to working with imperfect bosses is to get a wide and deep perspective on this topic of leadership. There is a wide variety of effective leaders out there. I've had the opportunity to minister in thirty-seven countries and to see and work with many Christian leaders. I'm always amazed at the variety of effective leaders. Some are too authoritarian for my taste. Some are too bookish, and some too prone to follow ministry fads. Others are way too loud, from my perspective. And yet God uses them all and they are effective. The book of Proverbs instructs us to "get understanding." Read up on the subject of leadership. Study the leaders in Scriptures. Our view of what makes an effective leader is usually too narrow when we are young.

Young ministers' estimation of the leaders that God uses to build His kingdom is often limited to what they experienced as they grew up. For example, I grew up thinking that the way to grow a great church was through great preaching. My image of a successful pastor was shaped by my experience in one church with one pastor. Later, as I worked with and observed other lead pastors, I became aware of the diversity of effective leaders. I was surprised to learn that leaders grow great churches through a variety of means such as great leadership, intense prayer, great faith, or great teamwork, and not just through great preaching.

How does this relate to dealing with the faults of bosses? The increased understanding of what makes an effective leader helps me see that God greatly uses leaders even with glaring faults and leaders with impure motives (does anyone have totally pure motives?). I understand that even though King David was both an adulterer and a murderer God used him in a great way. Moses was not perfect, nor was Peter, or Paul. Yet God used each of them in a unique way. God is not answerable to us regarding whom He chooses to use for His work. He is sovereign.

You may be surprised to see what God does through your boss. You know his faults, and yet you see results, sometimes great results. Rejoice! That should give you hope that God will use you, too, in spite of your faults.

The Temptation to Triangulate

One of the challenges for young ministers is learning how to overcome the obstacles to their projects. There are various kinds of obstacles, including financial shortages, lack of volunteers, and conflict. But a common obstacle for anyone considering a new ministry project is just getting the permission from the boss to move forward with their project. When the boss says "no" to a proposed ministry project, the young leader has a choice to make: Forget the project for now, or find some other way to get it approved. That second choice can create problems.

One way to "find some other way to get it approved" is by using triangulation. This is not a recommended method.

"Triangulation is getting your way by using a secondary authority to undermine a primary authority. It is doing a so-called 'end run' around others, bypassing corporate structure to achieve fast and sometimes risky results."[35]

Consider this story that is based on a true situation:

> Eli, a new associate in a para-church ministry, formulates a new project for the ministry. Eli shares his project idea with the executive director but the director rejects it, saying, "This is not the time for this project. But let's discuss it in the future." At that point, Eli should forget the project and move on. But, not willing to give up, Eli shares his project idea with other staff members. However, he does not tell them of the director's rejection of the idea. The other staff members like Eli's idea and verbally support it though they are unaware that it has already been vetoed. At the next staff meeting one of the staff members, not knowing that Eli has already discussed his idea with the director, asks Eli to share his project idea with the rest of the staff. Eli shares it. The other staff members, not knowing of the director's disapproval, are

generally behind Eli's idea. The Director firmly responds that he and Eli have already discussed this project idea but that this is not the time for it. Once again, he vetoes it. As a result of the whole process Eli's credibility with both his director and other staff members has been damaged. The director could interpret Eli's actions as attempting to triangulate. The staff members could be angry that Eli didn't inform them that the director had already vetoed his idea. Eli's relationship with his director and staff could easily be strained.

A variation of this story could be that the director feels so much pressure from the staff that he grudgingly approves the idea but within he is angry at Eli.

What are the results of triangulation? One of the positive aspects is that the person doing the triangulation is able to promote his or her agenda or program. The negative is that it undermines others and demonstrates disrespect toward a supervisor or leadership team.

There are two common arenas of triangulation:

1. An employee exerts influence or promotes a particular agenda over the head of another employee.
2. An employee combines strengths and resources with another employee to work an agenda apart from, or against, a supervisor. The employee creates an alliance to help him achieve his goal.[36]

In this chapter I am concerned primarily with the second common arena. I'm not saying that this method won't work in achieving the goal of accomplishing a task. It may work very well. The young leader may get his way, even against the wishes of his boss. But the question must be asked: At what cost?

I remember a time early in my ministry when I used triangulation to get my way. I'm not proud of this experience, but I'll share it so that you can read of a specific triangulation situation. It all started when I asked for permission to attend a national conference and my boss said no. The reason my boss gave was that I didn't have enough money in my work account to pay for the trip expenses (about $1,000), but I knew that wasn't true. I checked my work account balance and I had more than ten times the amount I needed for the trip. I concluded that my boss had another reason for declining, but I wasn't aware of what it was (I still don't know the reason).

To my shame, I didn't let it rest. I told my story to a friend. I had no idea that he served on a national committee and would take up my case. Without telling me my friend interceded for me and alerted the higher authorities about my boss's decision, and soon, to my surprise, I received permission to attend. At that point I should have called my boss to explain what had happened, apologize, and inform him that I would not attend the conference. However, I went to the conference. Only later did I stop and think, and realize that I had damaged my relationship with my boss.

Good leaders choose not to use triangulation in accomplishing a task. But sometimes young leaders don't think it through. They forge ahead with their ideas without thinking about the effect their actions may have on their relationship with others, particularly with their boss. It may be best to simply forget the ministry project and protect the relationship with your boss and others.

I don't mean to discourage young leaders from proposing and taking on ministry projects but we need to remember that it is possible to accomplish tasks without using triangulation. We must learn how to work within the constraints of our ministry, build relationships, and still accomplish tasks.

A key question that all Christian leaders must answer is whether they are willing to submit. Many who aspire to leadership fail because they have never learned to follow. This can be a difficult challenge for a young minister. It's easy to submit when you agree with the decision of your boss. It's difficult when you disagree with the decision. But when you submit in those circumstances you leave room for God to work out His will in other, unforeseen ways. Young ministers who learn to submit, even when they feel they are correct and have "evidence" to back up their claim, will have learned a valuable lesson.

Candid Dialogue

I think all leaders should cultivate within their organizations a healthy respect for debate where, when an issue is being considered, assistants have permission to express their views openly. In his book *Why Great Leaders Don't Take Yes For An Answer*, Michael A. Roberto argues that leaders best serve their organizations when they allow open debate on issues. Roberto states that former USA president John F. Kennedy could have avoided the Bay of Pigs crisis in 1961 if he'd sought out a wide variety of opinions on the impending crisis. Instead, he wouldn't listen to those who might disagree with him, and, as a result, the USA and Russia nearly launched a nuclear confrontation.

Roberto states, "One cannot discount the critical role that a particular leader's style and personality can play in encouraging or discouraging candid dialogue within an organization. Leadership does matter. Make no mistake about that."[37]

Does your boss encourage candid dialogue? Is there candid dialogue among staff in your ministry? What is it about your boss's style and personality that either encourages or discourages candid dialogue? And how about your relationship with your followers, how does your own leadership style and personality either promote or inhibit open dialogue with your leadership team?

The goal is not to have candid conversations for the sake of being candid. The goal is to have constructive conversations so that all issues are considered and good decisions are made.

What can you, as a young leader, do to encourage candid discussion? You can understand the nuances surrounding this issue. A nuance is a "fine distinction" on a subject. Following are some of those fine distinctions related to this topic.

Openness Varies by Topic

The key question is not so much, "Is my boss open to candid discussions?" as it is, "What does my boss think about open discussion on this topic?" Most likely, your boss's willingness to allow open discussion on a topic differs from topic to topic. You need to understand your boss and adjust your openness accordingly. There are times when you will broach a subject and find that your boss is closed to discussion on that topic. At other times, you might sense openness to candid discussion on a topic. You must use your judgment in each situation.

Comfort Is Not the Same as Toleration

The key is to appraise how much discussion, and perhaps disagreement, your boss is comfortable with. This is not the same as asking how much disagreement your boss can tolerate. Tolerating disagreement is one thing. Being comfortable with disagreements is another. Every person has a comfort threshold, an invisible line. If you "step over the line" or even approach that line, the discussion will probably shut down.

Affirm Loyalty, Then Understand the Ground Rules

I would recommend that in the early days of a new position, well before you've had the opportunity to disagree with your boss, you should find ways to affirm your loyalty to him. The most common way to do that is to tell your boss that one of your core values is loyalty. Once you've established your commitment to loyalty, then, at some point sit down and ask him how you should approach differences of opinion, should they arise. Ask him for the ground rules. Explain that you raised this issue because you want to be the best assistant he could ever have. Leaders are more open to candid discussions if they know their associates are loyal.

Good Days and Bad Days

Everybody has good days and bad days. Some days you welcome a good debate on a worthy topic, you're ready for anything. But on other days, you just want to make it through the work day, go home, and get some rest. Even the best bosses have good and bad days, and a wise associate will exercise judgment in launching a debate.

Two Cautions Regarding Candid Discussions

For your protection I want to raise two cautions. The first involves those who just graduated from college: Recent graduates do well to remember that that the atmosphere in college may differ remarkably from the atmosphere at their first place of ministry. In college, candid discussion in the classroom is often not only approved but encouraged. As a result, college students get into the habit of having candid discussions with a wide variety of people. But then they graduate and take a youth pastor position, expecting the same candid discussions to occur in their staff meetings, or individually with their boss. But, as I mentioned earlier, bosses (and colleagues) differ as to how much candid dialogue they will tolerate. Some youth pastors have damaged their trust and relationship with their senior leader by assuming that the "permission to speak openly" they enjoyed in college will carry over to their workplace. Sometimes it does; sometimes it doesn't.

The second caution is specifically for those who like to read leadership books and attend leadership workshops. I like to read, and I notice that there are many books that promote the virtues of a flat organizational flowchart and the blessings of open communication in organizations. I've heard workshop presenters say, "We're living in a new day. It's a day when leaders are committed to teamwork, flat organizational charts, and open discussion in staff meetings." Some young leaders take that input as permission to disagree openly and sometimes strongly with their boss during staff meetings. Other young leaders are not so open as that but still have an "edge" that their boss notices, and that edge causes the boss to throw up defenses against the debate and the young leader. The truth is that candid discussion within staff meetings is not as accepted as some books and workshop presenters proclaim. I hope that the first boss you work with is open to candid discussions but you never know until that time.

Fortunately, there are many bosses who seek out dissenting opinions when considering important issues. They earnestly want to hear both sides of the issue before making a decision. Roberto states: "Perhaps most importantly, leaders cannot wait for dissent to come to them; they must actively *go seek it out* in their organizations. If leaders offer personal invitations to others, requesting their opinions, ideas, and alternative viewpoints, they will find people becoming much more willing to speak freely and openly."[38]

Occasionally, I meet a young leader who is ready to quit due to major disagreements with his boss. For example, consider the actual case of a minister who I'll call Norm. Early in his ministry Norm took a position as assistant pastor under a lead pastor, Steve. Their priorities were quite different. Norm believed that the correct life priority order for ministers should be: God first, family second, and ministry third. But Steve, Norm's lead pastor, deliberately put ministry ahead of his own family.

Norm's reaction? "The main thing I remember Pastor Steve telling me was, 'Unless you put the church ahead of your family, you will never succeed in ministry.' I disagreed with that philosophy." Norm concluded,

"Due to Pastor Steve's philosophy of work before family, he messed up his family. Had I worked with him for years it would have been like selling my soul. So I quit."

When there is such a stark contrast between your own values and that of your boss, it may be advisable to quit. It's important to "draw the line" at certain points. But I believe that most disagreements we have with our bosses should not result in quitting. Many issues that seem important at the time look pretty insignificant in hindsight.

Questions for Young Leaders

1. How is your attitude toward your boss?

2. Can you think of an instance when you or a colleague used triangulation to get his/your way? What happened? What was the result?

3. What is it about your boss's style and personality that either encourages or discourages candid dialogue?

Questions for Lead Pastors or Ministry Directors

1. What ground rules could you give to your staff regarding disagreements with the boss?

2. Imagine a young assistant pastor who doesn't get along with his lead pastor. When is it time for an associate in that situation to leave, to quit? Is there a dividing line beyond which they just won't be able to work well together? If so, what is it?

3. How does a creative young leader exercise his creativity without being perceived as a maverick?

Benjamin M. Kaufman

Recommendations for Lead Pastors or Ministry Directors

1. Periodically ask your young leaders for feedback regarding your relationship with them. Invite discussion.

2. Lay out the ground rules for staff discussions. What is acceptable? What is not acceptable?

Challenge # 13

Staff Relationships

In 2005 I conducted a leadership workshop with a group of about twenty-five youth pastors. As part of that workshop, I asked them the following question: "What are the challenges of being a youth pastor or an assistant in a church?"

Following is a list of their responses that I wrote on the white board as they cited them. They are not in order of significance. There is an obvious overlap between the twelve challenges.

1. Dealing with the lead pastor's decisions that I do not agree with
2. How to serve the lead pastor
3. Incongruence of ministry vision between myself and the lead pastor
4. Budget allocations
5. Working with others on the pastoral staff (other assistant pastors)
6. Adjusting my communication style to the lead pastor
7. Keeping the lead pastor's concerns as my top priorities
8. Synchronizing with the lead pastor
9. Keeping "fire" from spreading. (Others in the church come to me with complaints about lead pastor and others on staff.)
10. Not saying too much (when others ask about things happening in the church)
11. I must defend the lead pastor even when I do not agree with him.
12. I must serve the lead pastor's vision.

Note: In the pages that follow, I use the words "assistant pastor" to mean any of the pastoral staff members who are not the lead pastor.

Assistant pastor signifies executive pastor, associate pastor, assistant pastor, youth pastor, music minister, children's pastor, or any other pastoral staff member.

After I listed their responses on the white board, I asked the youth pastors to highlight which of the twelve challenges are the most difficult. Sixty percent of the participants cited challenge #5, "working with others on the pastoral staff (other assistant pastors)" as the most difficult challenge. In other words, six out of every ten stated that working with fellow staff members was the most difficult challenge among the twelve they had cited.

That training session provides insight to a reality that has been given little attention: Some of the greatest challenges for assistant ministers are the relationships with their colleagues. When I thought about my own training for ministry—and when I asked Drew and Mike about their training—we remarked how little attention had been paid to those relationships in our training for ministry. We were not instructed regarding how to work well with our colleagues on a church staff.

Specifically, what are the challenges assistants face as they work with one another?

Building Trusting Relationships

A church or ministry staff is a team. And like any team the team members must trust one another if they are going to succeed. Sadly, some staffs are characterized more by suspicion than trust, by competition rather than cooperation, and by self-interest rather than love for one another.

There are many keys to building trusting relationships among team members but I want to focus on one—honoring and affirming one another. This key is basic but powerful.

We can honor our fellow staff members in a number of ways, not the least of which is to affirm them verbally in their contribution to the kingdom and to our lives. Simply put, let your fellow staff members know of your appreciation for them. Suspicion and a lack of trust can engulf your staff relationships when you are silent, when others don't know where you stand in relation to them. But when you express to them your loyalty, then suspicion and lack of trust find it more difficult to grow.

Proverbs 27:5 (NLT) says, "An open rebuke is better than hidden love!" I summarize that verse with two words, "Express it." Express your love and devotion to those with whom you work. When you think they have done a good job let them know.

Paul and his co-workers were affirmers. Paul wrote to the church at Thessalonica with these affirming words, "...we think of your faithful work, your loving deeds, and your continual anticipation of the return of our Lord Jesus Christ" (1 Thessalonians 1:3, NLT).

Paul also affirmed the church at Thessalonica when he was communicating with other churches. "We proudly tell God's other churches about your endurance and faithfulness..." (2 Thessalonians 1:4, NLT).

Consider this issue from another angle: How do you feel when others tell you that they appreciate you and your work? It creates a bond with them, doesn't it? Ask yourself if you are expressing the loyalty you feel in your heart toward your leader and fellow staff members.

As a staff member, if you practice this principle you will be part of the glue that holds together a ministry staff. And when others see you doing a good job they will most likely return the affirmation.

Dealing with Fellow Staff Members' Responses to Your Ideas

Young leaders sometimes complain that nobody listens seriously to their ideas. They present ideas in staff meetings and their ideas are not seriously considered whereas older staff members seem to get a genuine hearing.

I have no doubt that their complaint is generally true. Our culture has low esteem for "rookies." Older members commonly expect the younger ones to "earn their stripes." The attitude is, "Why should we listen to you? You're young." We could debate all day whether this attitude is correct, and why it occurs. But our strategy here is to deal with life as it is.

When your views are ignored, you have a variety of options available to you. You can...

+ Continue submitting ideas though you know others will not give them a fair hearing.

- ✦ Stop submitting ideas.
- ✦ Hold a grudge against those who don't listen to your ideas.
- ✦ Stop listening to the ideas of others. (They are not listening to you so why listen to them?)
- ✦ Quit the staff or leave the group.
- ✦ Adopt the strategy of building credibility so that eventually you are heard.

I recommend the last option.

There are several verses in Paul's first letter to Timothy that particularly apply to this challenge. You will recall that Paul wrote to Timothy, who was probably around the age of thirty at the time. Paul writes to Timothy about various responsibilities that Timothy should assume as he pastors the church in Ephesus, then Paul instructs, "Give your complete attention to these matters. Throw yourself into your tasks so that everyone will see your progress" (1 Tim. 4:15, NLT).

I find it interesting that Paul makes a point of wanting others to see Timothy's progress. Paul not only wants Timothy to make progress, he wants others to notice that Timothy is making progress. Why? I believe it's because others trust a young guy or gal in ministry whom they see is making progress. A young leader can do nothing about his or her age—if you are young and therefore don't have a lot of ministry experience, you can't change that immediately. But young leaders can make choices that cause them to develop and grow. When others see that development, their confidence in them grows.

Too often we want to move from a position of no credibility to a position of unlimited credibility. Wouldn't it be great to have the credibility of Joseph right now? Pharaoh said to Joseph, "You shall be in charge of my palace, and all my people are to submit to your orders. Only with respect to the throne will I be greater than you" (Genesis 41:40). That kind of credibility is rare, and when it exists, it has been earned over time.

The pathway to credibility is through service. In his book *Leading from the Second Chair*, Mike Bonem emphasizes the value of service.

> Building credibility and influence requires putting the prestige of your position aside and picking up the towel of service. You must commit to serving your entire

organization well, each and every day. Then, and only then, will your peers, subordinates, and senior leader truly allow you to lead from the second chair.[39]

Generational Differences

Chances are, you will face generational challenges when you are part of a ministry staff. Be prepared for them. They are one kind of challenge that you can count on.

In a meeting I had with a youth pastor, following a time of discussion on this subject of staff relationships, the youth pastor remarked on what he had seen among his friends. "The problems between lead pastor and young pastor were often the result of the age differences. They were not able to bridge the differences in perspectives."

The age differences surface not just between young and old but even among younger ministers. One young youth pastor, age twenty-eight, spoke of the new perspective that he gained from his relationship to another minister, age twenty-three, who had just been hired to work under him as an assistant youth pastor.

> At our church we just hired a twenty-three-year old on staff. There have been moments when I have been able to get a glimpse of how it feels to be the "old guy." I'm twenty-eight and he is twenty-three. He is the new junior high pastor and he answers to me. There are *moments* when he thinks that I'm really cool.

Generational differences can exist even within a generation.

Though there are obvious obstacles as different generations seek to work with one another, one strategy will reduce the power of those obstacles: Those in the various generations must have conversations with one another. They must learn from one another.

What can you do to encourage conversations between the generations?

Try to understand the "why." An important key is to understand why each generation is as they are. There are reasons that every generation differs. Each has been molded by experiences they had and people they

155

knew as they grew up. To the extent that those incidents have been experienced by a group of people born at about the same time, they are referred to as generational characteristics. When we know the experiences that have shaped a generation we more easily recognize the legitimacy of their beliefs.

One attribute of many who are part of the "builders" generation (those over age sixty-two) is that they are tight-fisted with their money. About ten years ago, my wife, Sherie, and I had breakfast with an eighty-year-old man and his wife, and he insisted on paying the bill. After he'd paid the bill, I offered to leave the tip but he insisted on paying the tip, too, and said he would leave it on the table. As we left the table I happened to glance back and see him place the tip on the table. It was a quarter. There were four of us at breakfast, each of us had ordered a meal, and he had left the waitress twenty-five cents. Talk about tight-fisted! Of course, I know that not all members of the "builders" generation leave small tips. Many are very generous with the waiter. But there is no question that most "builders" understand the value of money. Why? The older members of that generation grew up during the Great Depression when money was very hard to come by. If today's twenty-five-year-olds had grown up during such difficult financial times, they, too, would probably be known for being tight-fisted.

When you encounter opposition from a person of a different generation than your own, take some time to consider why they act as they do. Does it have to do with generational differences, to the experiences they had as they grew up? Taking time to understand will strengthen your relationship with the person.

Don't undervalue your contribution. Occasionally, I talk with a young minister who thinks he has little to contribute to his ministry or church because he is young and inexperienced. He may look at older ministers, think he does not measure up, and thus undervalue his prospective contribution. We older ministers are partly to blame for this viewpoint because we don't always appreciate the numerous good things young ministers bring to our ministries, and we don't tell them that we appreciate them. We too easily forget all the mistakes we made when we were young. By being mute we can strangle the prospective contributions of the younger generations. In contrast to that, Paul urged the church to accept young Timothy. Paul was using his influence to help Timothy achieve success. He knew that Timothy, like you, could make a great contribution to the Kingdom of God.

Watch out for reverse discrimination. In 1 Timothy 5:21 Paul warns against showing special favor. There is a tendency among ministers of all ages to favor the people of their own generation. I am fifty-five (I can't believe it) and easily see the legitimacy of the opinions of those in my age bracket. However, in regard to those who are twenty years older than me, or those who are twenty years younger, I don't quite see things as they do. There is a certain generational blindness to perspectives of other generations. This kind of blindness can be overcome. Paul writes to Timothy, "I solemnly command you in the presence of God and Christ Jesus and the holy angels to obey these instructions *without taking sides or showing special favor to anyone*" (1 Tim. 5:21, NLT, italics added).

I remember talking to a church consultant who related the following story. He had consulted at a church where all the staff members were age thirty-five and under, including the lead pastor. In their staff meeting the staff members were congratulating themselves on being a church that was open to all kinds of ideas and that did not have the narrow view of some older church staffs. The unspoken thought was that since they were a young staff, they had a wide-open perspective. The consultant spoke up and reminded them that if they truly wanted to be open in perspective, they might consider including an older person on their staff. He reasoned that it is not just the younger crowd that has new and good ideas. He concluded that they were closed to many ideas simply because they, too, just as many groups of older ministers, had a narrow generational perspective.

Remember that other generations are not your adversaries. With all the talk about generational differences, it is easy to slip into an implicit adversarial approach. We don't even realize we are doing it. Our culture "sets up" teenagers to be at odds with their parents and others over forty. Many young people assume that the older generation is out of touch and sees only from a narrow perspective. I refer to this as an implicit adversarial approach because it is not explicit—no minister just comes out and refers to those who are twenty years older as their adversaries. But there is no question that in American culture this mindset exists. This mindset can carry over into the ministry and the young minister may not even realize that he is carrying this perspective around with him.

The Scriptures provide a way to think about those from differing generations—a view that is just as relevant today as it was when it was written nearly 2,000 years ago.

> Never speak harshly to an older man, but appeal to him respectfully as though he were your own father. Talk to the younger men as you would to your own brothers. Treat the older women as you would your mother, and treat the younger women with all purity as your own sisters (1 Tim. 5:1-2, NLT).

These verses provide a perspective that contrasts with the adversarial approach toward other generations. These verses provide ways of thinking about other generations that builds bridges to them. With each group, Paul offers an approach and a set of behavioral expectations that encourages communication.

Conversations about Other Staff Members

Consider carefully what you say to others about your fellow staff members. You may have pure motives but once those words leave your mouth you don't know what others will do with them. Take a moment and reflect on those times when you've been hanging out with your young minister friends: What have you said about your fellow staff members? What attitude have you conveyed toward your fellow staff members?

Following are some conversation guidelines:

1. When "talking shop" about the ministry with friends, be careful. A little bird may take what you say and tell your fellow staff members. (Ecclesiastes 10:20)

2. Don't assume that what you say with friends will never be said again. Your friends probably don't mean to hurt you by repeating what you say. They may just speak without thinking. You may have good judgment but that doesn't mean that they have good judgment and know when to keep their mouths closed.

3. If you feel you've been mistreated by your fellow staff members but you've gotten over it, and you feel no bitterness about it, still, be careful. You may be able to talk about being mistreated with no hint of bitterness within you, but when you tell your "mistreatment story" to your colleagues, you may be unwittingly encouraging them to become bitter or cynical about working with their colleagues. Your intentions may be pure, but the content of what you say may hinder others who are experiencing conflict with their colleagues. One way to counter the negative is to include stories of the good things your colleagues do, too.

4. Find safe people with whom to discuss your relationship with your senior leader. For example, many church groups have regional youth directors and they are normally safe people to talk to. They are your advocates. To be safe, it is best if your confidant is outside your immediate ministry context.

5. Identify the people in your church or ministry who seem to love to stir up trouble. Be extra careful when talking to them. Say nothing to them that could be considered negative.

Be an Example among the Staff

I include this principle here because Paul emphasized it in his letter to Timothy. Though you are young, be an example. Take the lead in modeling biblical behavior. One youth pastor told me that his lead pastor had a habit of talking negatively about others in the church. The youth pastor was careful not to do the same. He was a positive example.

Note Paul's instructions to Timothy in 1 Timothy 4:12 (NLT): "Don't let anyone think less of you because you are young. Be an example to all believers in what you teach, in the way you live, in your love, your faith, and your purity."

Occasionally there will be a fellow staff member who has a toxic attitude. You must be careful that the attitude of toxic staff members doesn't poison you. Again, Paul's words to Timothy are relevant: "Keep a close watch on yourself and on your teaching. Stay true to what is right, and God will save you and those who hear you" (1 Tim. 4:16). Most staff members will possess a good attitude, but occasionally there will be one who has a toxic attitude. Be a godly example to him or her. Don't let that person influence you.

Finding Mentors on a Ministry Staff

Every leader needs people he can confide in and learn from. Clinton states, "Most of our leadership case studies identified between three and twenty (or sometimes more) people who were a significant part of the leader's development."[40]

In my interviews with leaders I discovered that many young ministers want to work with a lead pastor who is not only their boss but also is a friend with whom they can discuss ministry matters informally. One youth pastor, who deeply values the friendship he has with his lead pastor, advises prospective youth pastors to assign the lead pastor/youth pastor relationship as "high priority" when considering what lead pastor to work with. In fact, he recommends that when interviewing for a job, that the prospective youth pastor should ask the lead pastor what kind of lead pastor/youth minister relationship they will have, even before asking about salary issues.

But young leaders should not restrict their search for mentors to just the lead pastor. One experienced leader, who has been part of several church staffs, recommends that young ministers find mentors among the colleagues they serve with on staff: "Through the years I've needed to air things with my colleagues on staff. I felt I needed someone who understood."

As you look for mentors in the ministry, keep the following truths in mind:

- Remember that every relationship has limitations.
  Some leaders will have no interest in mentoring you no matter what you do to encourage those kinds of behaviors.

- Don't overestimate what you can expect from a mentor.
  Look for specific qualities or competencies in others and ask them to mentor you in those qualities or competencies. Don't expect

your mentor to help you in all areas of your work. Everyone has strengths; capitalize on your mentors' strengths.

+ Take the initiative.
  Ask the person to mentor you. If you wait for them to take the initiative, you may be waiting forever.

+ Be specific and set a time limit.
  Spell out specifically how often you want to meet and how long the meetings will be.

+ Take the prospective mentor out to lunch, or for coffee, and pick up the tab.
  Make it worthwhile for him. Take him to lunch for one or more of your coaching mentoring meetings. Or, meet at a coffee shop and pay for his coffee.

An important question to ask is, "What kind of person should I look for as my mentor?"

In *The Mentor Handbook*, Robert Clinton cites six characteristics to look for in a mentor:

1. Ability to readily see potential in a person
2. Tolerance with mistakes, brashness, abrasiveness and the like in order to see that potential develop
3. Flexibility: the ability to give and take and flow with a situation
4. Patience: knowing that time and experience are needed for development
5. Perspective: having vision and the ability to see down the road and suggest next steps that a mentoree needs
6. A gift-mix, including one or more of the encouragement spiritual gifts: mercy, giving, exhortation, teaching, faith, word of wisdom[41]

Sometimes, mentors have a difficult time with the give and take in a mentoring relationship. A great resource that will help mentors and leaders in this regard is Earl Crep's book, *Reverse Mentoring*. He provides great ideas for ways that young and older people can work together in a mentoring type relationship.

Watch Your Allegiances

Don't be overly devoted to a specific fellow staff member. Healthy respect is good and necessary but be careful that your allegiance to any one staff member is not too strong. You will naturally be drawn to some colleagues over others but keep some balance in this.

I don't mean that you shouldn't have people in whom you trust and confide more than others. Jesus Christ had various levels in his relationships, having Peter, James, and John within his inner circle. But, even so, when the mother of James and John came to request a special place in God's kingdom Jesus was quick to put them in place. Jesus did not sacrifice the wider kingdom principles by his allegiances.

Allegiances are often highlighted in conflict situations. Other leaders, including the senior leader and staff members, may encourage you to take sides when there is a conflict. You should be cautious in these situations and take a stand for kingdom principles, above all.

Consider what Paul had to say in 1 Corinthians 4:6: "Dear brothers and sisters, I have used Apollos and myself to illustrate what I've been saying. If you pay attention to the Scriptures, you won't brag about one of your leaders at the expense of another."

I like what the Life Application Bible has to say on this verse:

> How easy it is for us to become attached to a spiritual leader. When someone has helped us, it's natural to feel loyalty. But Paul warns against having such pride in our favorite leaders that we cause divisions in the church. Any true spiritual leader is a representative of Christ and has nothing to offer that God hasn't given him or her. Don't let your loyalty cause strife, slander, or broken relationships.[42]

That is a good word for all ministers, particularly for young leaders.

Questions for Young Leaders

1. How would you respond to this question I posed to the group of youth pastors in 2005: "What are the challenges of being a youth pastor or an assistant in a church?"

2. When others pay little attention to you and your views, how do you normally react? How should you react?

3. What is the greatest challenge you encounter in your relationships with colleagues and other people who are older than you?

4. Do you have someone who works with you on staff who could be a mentor to you? If so, what are that person's strengths? Develop a short plan for arranging the mentoring with him/her, including the following:
   - What do you want to discuss with him/her?
   - How many meetings do you want to set up with him/her?
   - How often will you meet with this person as your mentor?

Questions for Lead Pastors or Ministry Directors

1. From your experience, what are the most difficult challenges facing young leaders who are part of a church or ministry staff?

2. How do you cultivate affirming relationships among your staff?

3. What advice would you give to young staff members who feel that others are not listening to their ideas?

4. I provided some conversation guidelines for young ministers so that they don't hurt their relationships with fellow staff members. What guidelines would you add that would help the young ministers develop trusting relationships with their colleagues?

5. Have you seen staff members develop unhealthy allegiances with fellow staff members? If so, what have been the causes and results of those allegiances?

Recommendations for Lead Pastors or Ministry Directors

1. With your staff, develop a workshop outline titled, "How to Build Trusting Relationships among Staff Members." Include the following points in the outline:
    *   Why build trusting relationships?
    *   What tears down trusting relationships?
    *   What are the top ten keys to developing trusting relationships among staff members?

2. Lead the following affirmation exercise during a staff meeting:

    Choose one team member and have all the other team members answer this question about the person: What is one characteristic this team member has, or one behavior that this team member does, that helps this team be effective? Once all team members have affirmed that person, do the same for all other team members.

Final Thoughts

Two kingdom principles will help us we face the various challenges in the early years of ministry. One is to see life as a test, and the other is to see the challenges as God's method of shaping us into His image.

In *The Purpose Driven Life*, Rick Warren states that life is a test, a trust, and a temporary assignment.[43] I want to focus on this idea that life is a test. This is a healthy way to view your challenges—as tests. They are there to be overcome with the power of God in your life. If you don't pass your tests, God will still love you, of course, but He is looking for those who are faithful with what He has given them. Remember Jesus' words to the wise investor, recorded in the Gospel of Matthew. "The master was full of praise. 'Well done, my good and faithful servant. You have been faithful in handling this small amount, so now I will give you many more responsibilities. Let's celebrate together!' " (Matthew 25:21, NLT). That investor passed the test.

As you face the challenges of your early ministry years you'll be better able to navigate them if you see them as tests from God, tests that God wants you to pass and will help you pass.

The second principle that will motivate us as we face our challenges is the shaping concept. God is shaping us to be His servants. We must allow Him to do His work in us.

Consider what the Lord spoke to Jeremiah.

> The Lord gave another message to Jeremiah. He said, "Go down to the shop where clay pots and jars are made. I will speak to you while you are there." So I did as he told me and found the potter working at his wheel. But the jar he was making did not turn out as he had hoped,

165

so the potter squashed the jar into a lump of clay and started again. Then the Lord gave me this message: "O Israel, can I not do to you as this potter has done to his clay? As the clay is in the potter's hand, so are you in my hand." (Jeremiah 18:1-6, NLT)

We must stay on the wheel and let God shape us. Consider Moses as an example. More than once Moses was ready to get off that wheel and run away. But he didn't. He put up with all of those people when they were disobedient and complaining and he allowed God to shape him in the midst of conflict.

I encourage you to see ministry challenges as part of God's shaping process in your life. Stay on the potter's wheel and let Him develop you!

About The Author

◦

Dr. Benjamin M. Kaufman is founder and director of Leadership Development Ministries, a coaching and leadership training ministry based in San Juan Capistrano, California. In thirty-two years of full-time ministry he has served in a variety of ministry positions, including youth pastor, lead pastor, consultant, and missionary. He is inspired by the words spoken of the Old Testament patriarch Job, of whom it was said, "Your words have put men on their feet" (Job 4:4). Through his coaching, training, and writing, Ben strives to help ministers persevere and remain effectively engaged in ministry.

For further information see the website: www.FlourishingInTheMinistry.com

Endnotes

1 Dean R. Hoge & Jacqueline E. Wenger, *Pastors in Transition: Why Clergy Leave Local Church Ministry*, Grand Rapids, MI: Eerdmans Publishing Company, 2005, pp. 161-162.

2 Ibid, p. 162.

3 Doug Fields, *Your First Two Years in Youth Ministry: A Personal and Practical Guide to Starting Right*, Zondervan: Grand Rapids, MI and Youth Specialties Books: El Cajon, CA, 2002, p. 48.

4 *Pastors in Transition*, p. 160.

5 *Pastors in Transition*, p. 159.

6 *Pastors in Transition*, p. 159.

7 S. R. Bierly, *How to Thrive as a Small-Church Pastor: A Guide to Spiritual and Emotional Well-Being*, Grand Rapids, MI: Zondervan Publishing House, 1998, p. 138.

8 Fields, *Your First Two Years in Youth Ministry: A Personal and Practical Guide to Starting Right*, pp. 97-98.

9 Benjamin Kaufman, *Pressing On! Why Leaders Derail and What to Do about It*, Enumclaw, WA: Winepress Publishers 2004, p. 15.

10 Fields, *Your First Two Years in Youth Ministry: A Personal and Practical Guide to Starting Right*, p.57.

11 S. M. R. Covey, with Merrill, R. R., *The Speed of Trust: The One Thing that Changes Everything*, New York: Free Press, 2005, p. 43.

12 *Life Application Bible: New Living Translation*, Wheaton, IL: Tyndale House Publishers, Inc., 1996, p. 89.

13 D. R. Hoge & J.E. Wenger, *Pastors in Transition: Why Clergy Leave Local Church Ministry*, Grand Rapids, MI: Eerdmans Publishing Company, 2005, pp. 15-17.

14 Michael Dobson, & Deborah Singer Dobson, *Enlightened Office Politics. Understanding, Coping with, and Winning the Game —Without Losing Your Soul*, New York: Amacom: 2001, p. 4.

15 Richard M. Nixon, *Leaders*, New York, NY: Warner Books, 1982, p. 324.

16 M.W. McCall, M.M Lombardo, and A.M. Morrison, *The Lessons of Experience. How Successful Executives Develop on the Job*, New York: The Free Press, 1988, p. 78.

[17] J. Robert Clinton, *The Making of a Leader: Recognizing the Lessons and Stages of Leadership Development*, Colorado Springs, CO: Navpress, 1988, p. 109.

[18] Ibid, pp. 109-110.

[19] Adapted from Bobby Clinton & Richard Clinton, *The Mentor Handbook: Detailed Guidelines and Helps for Christian Mentors and Mentorees*, Altadena, CA: Barnabas Publishers, 1991, p. 8-5.

[20] Douglas L. Fagerstrom, *The Ministry Staff Member: A Contemporary, Practical Handbook to Equip, Encourage, and Empower*, Grand Rapids, MI: Zondervan, 2006, pp. 194-195.

[21] Bobby Clinton & Richard Clinton, *The Mentor Handbook: Detailed Guidelines and Helps for Christian Mentors and Mentorees*, Altadena, CA: Barnabas Publishers, 1991, p. 8-5.

[22] Ibid, p. 8-7.

[23] J. Robert Clinton, *The Making of a Leader: Recognizing the Lessons and Stages of Leadership Development*, Colorado Springs, CO: Navpress, 1988, p. 136

[24] Ibid, p. 138.

[25] Bobby Clinton & Richard Clinton, *The Mentor Handbook: Detailed Guidelines and Helps for Christian Mentors and Mentorees*, Altadena, CA: Barnabas Publishers, 1991, p. 2-3.

[26] Daniel Goleman, Richard Boytzis, and Annie McKee, *Primal Leadership: Learning to Lead with Emotional Intelligence*, Boston: Harvard Business School Press, 2002, p. 63.

[27] Gary L. McIntosh, & Samuel D. Rima, *Overcoming the Dark Side of Leadership: The Paradox of Personal Dysfunction*, Grand Rapids, MI: Baker Books, 1997, p. 22.

[28] Ibid, p. 22.

[29] Ibid, pp. 12-13.

[30] Chapter, "Managing Your Boss" from the book, *Leadership: Understanding the Dynamics of Power and Influence in Organizations*, by Robert P. Vecchio, Editor, Notre Dame, Indiana: University of Notre Dame Press, p. 100.

[31] Ibid, p. 100.

[32] Ibid, p. 100.

[33] Aubrey Malphurs, *Advanced Strategic Planning: A New Model for Church and Ministry Leaders*, Grand Rapids, MI: Baker Books 2005, p. 85.

[34] Adapted from "Creating the Right Leadership Culture," H. Finzel, in *Leaders on Leadership: Wisdom, Advice, and Encouragement on the Art of Leading God's People*, Barna, Ventura, CA: Regal Books, 1997, p. 271.

[35] Douglas L. Fagerstrom *The Ministry Staff Member: A Contemporary, Practical Handbook to Equip, Encourage, and Empowe*, Grand Rapids, MI: Zondervan, 2006, p. 88.

[36] Ibid, p. 89.

[37] Michael A. Roberto, *Why Great Leaders Don't Take Yes for an Answer: Managing for Conflict and Consensus*, Upper Saddle River, New Jersey: Wharton School Publishing, 2005, p. 83.

[38] Ibid, p. 83.

[39] Mike Bonem & Roger Patterson, *Leading from the Second Chair: Serving Your*

Church, Fulfilling Your Role, and Realizing Your Dreams, San Francisco, CA: Jossey-Bass, 2005, p. 13.

40 Bobby Clinton & Richard Clinton, *The Mentor Handbook: Detailed Guidelines and Helps for Christian Mentors and Mentorees*, Altadena, CA: Barnabas Publishers, 1991, p. 2-2.

41 Ibid, p. 2-2.

42 *Life Application Bible: New Living Translation*, Wheaton, IL: Tyndale House Publishers, Inc., 1996, p. 1806.

43 Rick Warren, *The Purpose Driven Life: What on Earth am I Here For?* Manila, Philippines: OMF Literature Inc., 2002, pp. 44-52.

CPSIA information can be obtained at www.ICGtesting.com
Printed in the USA
LVOW061812010412

275522LV00001B/17/P

9 781449 734183